I0410367

Congressional Research Service

Informing the legislative debate since 1914 _____

U.S. Strategic Nuclear Forces:
Background, Developments, and Issues

Amy F. Woolf

Specialist in Nuclear Weapons Policy

September 5, 2014

Congressional Research Service

7-5700

www.crs.gov

RL33640

Summary

Even though the United States plans to reduce the number of warheads deployed on its long-range missiles and bombers, consistent with the terms of the New START Treaty, it also plans to develop new delivery systems for deployment over the next 20-30 years. The 113th Congress will continue to review these programs during the annual authorization and appropriations process.

During the Cold War, the U.S. nuclear arsenal contained many types of delivery vehicles for nuclear weapons. The longer-range systems, which included long-range missiles based on U.S. territory, long-range missiles based on submarines, and heavy bombers that could threaten Soviet targets from their bases in the United States, are known as strategic nuclear delivery vehicles. At the end of the Cold War, in 1991, the United States deployed more than 10,000 warheads on these delivery vehicles. That number has declined to less than 2,000 warheads today, and is slated to decline to 1,550 warheads by 2018, after the New START Treaty completes implementation.

At the present time, the U.S. land-based ballistic missile force (ICBMs) consists of 450 Minuteman III ICBMs, each deployed with one warhead. The fleet will decline to 400 deployed missiles, while retaining all 450 launchers, to meet the terms of the New START Treaty. The Air Force is also modernizing the Minuteman missiles, replacing and upgrading their rocket motors, guidance systems, and other components, so that they can remain in the force through 2030. It is considering what to do to sustain or replace the missiles after 2030.

The U.S. ballistic missile submarine fleet currently consists of 14 Trident submarines; each carries 24 Trident II (D-5) missiles. The Navy converted 4 of the original 18 Trident submarines to carry non-nuclear cruise missiles. The remaining submarines currently carry around 1,000 warheads in total; that number will decline as the United States implements the New START Treaty. The Navy has shifted the basing of the submarines, so that nine are deployed in the Pacific Ocean and five are in the Atlantic, to better cover targets in and around Asia. It also has undertaken efforts to extend the life of the missiles and warheads so that they and the submarines can remain in the fleet past 2020. It is designing a new submarine and will replace the existing fleet beginning in 2031.

The U.S. fleet of heavy bombers includes 20 B-2 bombers and 78 B-52 bombers. The B-1 bomber is no longer equipped for nuclear missions. The fleet will decline to around 60 aircraft in coming years, as the United States implements New START. The Air Force has also begun to retire the nuclear-armed cruise missiles carried by B-52 bombers, leaving only about half the B-52 fleet equipped to carry nuclear weapons. The Air Force plans to procure both a new long-range bomber during the 2020s and a new cruise missile after 2030.

The Obama Administration completed a review of the size and structure of the U.S. nuclear force, and a review of U.S. nuclear employment policy, in June 2013. This review has advised the force structure that the United States will deploy under the New START Treaty. It is currently implementing the New START Treaty, with the reductions due to be completed by 2018. Congress will review the Administration's plans for U.S. strategic nuclear forces during the annual authorization and appropriations process, and as it assesses U.S. plans under New START and possible future arms control treaties with Russia. This report will be updated as needed.

Contents

Figures

Tables

Contacts

Introduction

During the Cold War, the U.S. nuclear arsenal contained many types of delivery vehicles for nuclear weapons, including short-range missiles and artillery for use on the battlefield, medium-range missiles and aircraft that could strike targets beyond the theater of battle, short- and medium-range systems based on surface ships, long-range missiles based on U.S. territory and submarines, and heavy bombers that could threaten Soviet targets from their bases in the United States. The short- and medium-range systems are considered non-strategic nuclear weapons and have been referred to as battlefield, tactical, and theater nuclear weapons.[1] The long-range missiles and heavy bombers are known as strategic nuclear delivery vehicles.

In 1990, as the Cold War was drawing to a close and the Soviet Union was entering its final year, the United States had more than 12,000 nuclear warheads deployed on 1,875 strategic nuclear delivery vehicles.[2] As of July 1, 2009, according to the counting rules in the Strategic Arms Reduction Treaty (START), the United States had reduced to 5,916 nuclear warheads on 1,188 strategic nuclear delivery vehicles.[3] Under the terms of the 2002 Strategic Offensive Reduction Treaty (known as the Moscow Treaty) between the United States and Russia, this number was to decline to no more than 2,200 operationally deployed strategic nuclear warheads by the end of 2012. The State Department reported that the United States has already reached that level, with only 1,968 operationally deployed strategic warheads in December 2009.[4] The New START Treaty, signed by President Obama and President Medvedev on April 8, 2010, reduces those forces further, to no more than 1,550 warheads on deployed launchers and heavy bombers.[5] According to the April 1, 2013, data exchange under that treaty, the United States now has 1,585 warheads on 778 deployed ICBMs, SLBMs, and heavy bombers.[6]

Although these numbers do not count the same categories of nuclear weapons, they indicate that the number of deployed warheads on U.S. strategic nuclear forces has declined significantly in the two decades following the end of the Cold War. Yet, nuclear weapons continue to play a key role in U.S. national security strategy, and the United States does not, at this time, plan to either eliminate its nuclear weapons or abandon the strategy of nuclear deterrence that has served as a core concept in U.S. national security strategy for more than 60 years. In a speech in Prague on April 5, 2009, President Obama highlighted "America's commitment to seek the peace and security of a world without nuclear weapons." But he recognized that this goal would not be

---

[1] For a detailed review of U.S. nonstrategic nuclear weapons see, CRS Report RL32572, *Nonstrategic Nuclear Weapons*, by Amy F. Woolf.

[2] Natural Resources Defense Council. Table of U.S. Strategic Offensive Force Loadings. Archive of Nuclear Data. http://www.nrdc.org/nuclear/nudb/datab1.asp The same source indicates that the Soviet Union, in 1990, had just over 11,000 warheads on 2,332 strategic nuclear delivery vehicles.

[3] Russia, by the same accounting, had 3,909 warheads on 814 delivery vehicles. See U.S. Department of State, Bureau of Verification, Compliance and Inspection. Fact Sheet. START Aggregate Numbers of Strategic Offensive Weapons. October 1, 2009. Washington, DC.

[4] U.S. State Department, Bureau of Public Affairs, *The Nuclear Nonproliferation Treaty: Promoting Disarmament*, Washington, DC, April 27, 2010, http://www.state.gov/documents/organization/141497.pdf.

[5] The parties are to meet this limit within seven years of entry-into-force, which could occur in early 2011. For more information on the New START Treaty, see CRS Report R41219, *The New START Treaty: Central Limits and Key Provisions*, by Amy F. Woolf.

[6] U.S. Department of State, Bureau of Arms Control, Verification, and Compliance, *New START Treaty Aggregate Numbers of Strategic Offensive Arms*, Fact Sheet, Washington, DC, April 1, 2014, http://www.state.gov/t/avc/rls/224236 htm.

reached quickly, and probably not in his lifetime.[7] And, even though the President pledged to reduce the roles and numbers of U.S. nuclear forces, the 2010 Nuclear Posture Review noted that "the fundamental role of U.S. nuclear weapons, which will continue as long as nuclear weapons exist, is to deter nuclear attack on the United States, our allies, and partners."[8] Moreover, in the 2010 NPR and in the June 2013 Report on the Nuclear Employment Guidance of the United States,[9] the Administration has indicated that the United States is planning to pursue programs that will allow it to modernize and adjust its strategic forces so that they remain capable in coming years.

This report reviews the ongoing programs that will affect the expected size and shape of the U.S. strategic nuclear force structure. It begins with an overview of this force structure during the Cold War, and summarizes the reductions and changes that have occurred since 1991. It then offers details about each category of delivery vehicle—land-based intercontinental ballistic missiles (ICBMs), submarine launched ballistic missiles (SLBMs), and heavy bombers—focusing on their current deployments and ongoing and planned modernization programs. The report concludes with a discussion of issues related to decisions about the future size and shape of the U.S. strategic nuclear force.

Background: The Strategic Triad

Force Structure and Size During the Cold War

Since the early 1960s the United States has maintained a "triad" of strategic nuclear delivery vehicles. The United States first developed these three types of nuclear delivery vehicles, in large part, because each of the military services wanted to play a role in the U.S. nuclear arsenal. However, during the 1960s and 1970s, analysts developed a more reasoned rationale for the nuclear "triad." They argued that these different basing modes had complementary strengths and weaknesses. They would enhance deterrence and discourage a Soviet first strike because they complicated Soviet attack planning and ensured the survivability of a significant portion of the U.S. force in the event of a Soviet first strike.[10] The different characteristics might also strengthen the credibility of U.S. targeting strategy. For example, ICBMs eventually had the accuracy and prompt responsiveness needed to attack hardened targets such as Soviet command posts and ICBM silos, SLBMs had the survivability needed to complicate Soviet efforts to launch a disarming first strike and to retaliate if such an attack were attempted,[11] and heavy bombers could be dispersed quickly and launched to enhance their survivability, and they could be recalled to their bases if a crisis did not escalate into conflict.

---

[7] The White House, Office of the Press Secretary, *Remarks by President Obama*, Prague, Czech Republic, April 5, 2009, http://www.whitehouse.gov/the_press_office/Remarks-By-President-Barack-Obama-In-Prague-As-Delivered/.

[8] U.S. Department of Defense, *Nuclear Posture Review*, Washington, DC, April 6, 2010, p. 15. http://www.defense.gov/npr/docs/2010%20Nuclear%20Posture%20Review%20Report.pdf.

[9] http://www.defense.gov/pubs/ReporttoCongressonUSNuclearEmploymentStrategy_Section491.pdf.

[10] U.S. Department of Defense. *Annual Report to Congress, Fiscal Year 1989*, by Frank Carlucci, Secretary of Defense. February 18, 1988. Washington, 1988. p. 54.

[11] In the early 1990s, SLBMs also acquired the accuracy needed to attack many hardened sites in the former Soviet Union.

According to unclassified estimates, the number of delivery vehicles (ICBMs, SLBMs, and nuclear-capable bombers) in the U.S. force structure grew steadily through the mid-1960s, with the greatest number of delivery vehicles, 2,268, deployed in 1967.[12] The number then held relatively steady through 1990, at between 1,875 and 2,200 ICBMs, SLBMs, and heavy bombers. The number of warheads carried on these delivery vehicles increased sharply through 1975, then, after a brief pause, again rose sharply in the early 1980s, peaking at around 13,600 warheads in 1987. **Figure 1** displays the increases in delivery vehicles and warheads between 1960, when the United States first began to deploy ICBMs, and 1990, the year before the United States and Soviet Union signed the first Strategic Arms Reduction Treaty (START).

Figure 1. U.S. Strategic Nuclear Weapons: 1960-1990

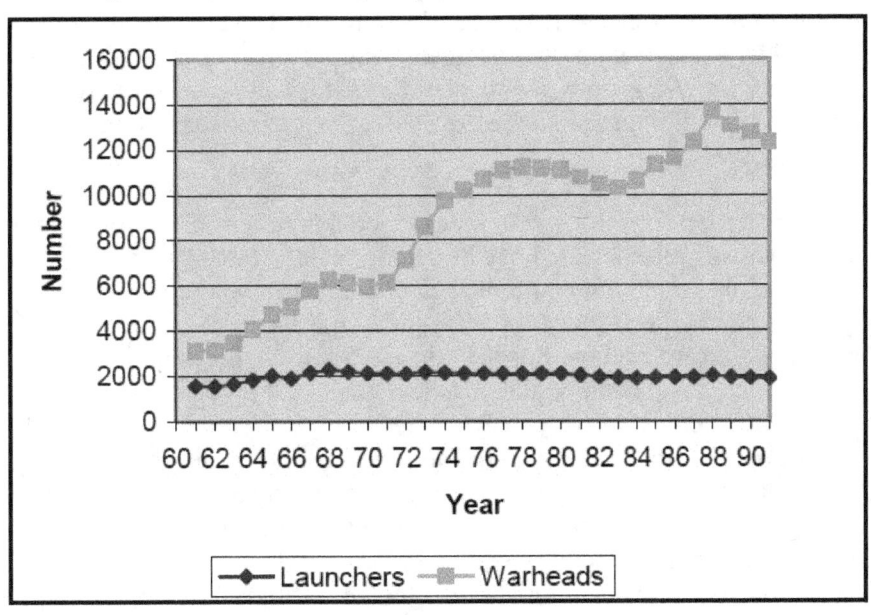

Source: Natural Resources Defense Council, Archive of Nuclear Data.

The sharp increase in warheads in the early 1970s reflects the deployment of ICBMs and SLBMs with multiple warheads, known as MIRVs (multiple independent reentry vehicles). In particular, the United States began to deploy the Minuteman III ICBM, with 3 warheads on each missile, in 1970, and the Poseidon SLBM, which could carry 10 warheads on each missile, in 1971.[13] The increase in warheads in the mid-1980s reflects the deployment of the Peacekeeper (MX) ICBM, which carried 10 warheads on each missile.

In 1990, before it concluded the START Treaty with the Soviet Union, the United States deployed a total of around 12,304 warheads on its ICBMs, SLBMs, and heavy bombers. The ICBM force consisted of single-warhead Minuteman II missiles, 3-warhead Minuteman III missiles, and 10-warhead Peacekeeper (MX) missiles, for a total force of 2,450 warheads on 1,000 missiles. The submarine force included Poseidon submarines with Poseidon C-3 and Trident I (C-4) missiles, and the Ohio-class Trident submarines with Trident I, and some Trident II (D-5) missiles. The

---

[12] Natural Resources Defense Council. Table of U.S. Strategic Offensive Force Loadings. Archive of Nuclear Data. http://www.nrdc.org/nuclear/nudb/datab1.asp.

[13] GlobalSecurity.org LGM Minuteman III History and Poseidon C-3 History. http://www.globalsecurity.org/wmd/systems/lgm-30_3-hist.htm and http://www.globalsecurity.org/wmd/systems/c-3.htm.

total force consisted of 5,216 warheads on around 600 missiles.[14] The bomber force centered on 94 B-52H bombers and 96 B-1 bombers, along with many of the older B-52G bombers and 2 of the new (at the time) B-2 bombers. This force of 260 bombers could carry over 4,648 weapons.

Force Structure and Size After the Cold War

During the 1990s, the United States reduced the numbers and types of weapons in its strategic nuclear arsenal, both as a part of its modernization process and in response to the limits in the 1991 START Treaty. The United States continued to maintain a triad of strategic nuclear forces, however, with warheads deployed on ICBMs, SLBMs, and bombers. According to the Department of Defense, this mix of forces not only offered the United States a range of capabilities and flexibility in nuclear planning and complicated an adversary's attack planning, but also hedged against unexpected problems in any single delivery system. This latter issue became more of a concern in this time period, as the United States retired many of the different types of warheads and missiles that it had deployed over the years, reducing the redundancy in its force.

The 1991 START Treaty limited the United States to a maximum of 6,000 total warheads, and 4,900 warheads on ballistic missiles, deployed on up to 1,600 strategic offensive delivery vehicles. However, the treaty did not count the actual number of warheads deployed on each type of ballistic missile or bomber. Instead, it used "counting rules" to determine how many warheads would count against the treaty's limits. For ICBMs and SLBMs, this number usually equaled the actual number of warheads deployed on the missile. Bombers, however, used a different system. Bombers that were not equipped to carry air-launched cruise missiles (the B-1 and B-2 bombers) counted as one warhead; bombers equipped to carry air-launched cruise missiles (B-52 bombers) could carry 20 missiles, but would only count as 10 warheads against the treaty limits. These rules have led to differing estimates of the numbers of warheads on U.S. strategic nuclear forces during the 1990s; some estimates count only those warheads that count against the treaty while others count all the warheads that could be carried by the deployed delivery systems.

According to the data from the Natural Resources Defense Council, the United States reduced its nuclear weapons from 9,300 warheads on 1,239 delivery vehicles in 1991 to 6,196 warheads on 1,064 delivery vehicles when it completed the implementation of START in 2001. By 2009, the United States had reduced its forces to approximately 2,200 warheads on around 850 delivery vehicles. According to the State Department, as of December 2009, the United States had 1,968 operationally deployed warheads on its strategic offensive nuclear forces.[15] NRDC estimated that these numbers held steady in 2010, prior to New START's entry into force, then began to decline again, falling to around 1,922 warheads on 851 delivery vehicles by early 2014, as the United States began to implement New START (this total includes weapons that the State Department does not count in the New START force). These numbers appear in **Figure 2**.

---

[14] The older Poseidon submarines were in the process of being retired, and the number of missiles and warheads in the submarine fleet dropped quickly in the early 1990s, to around 2,688 warheads on 336 missiles by 1993. See Natural Resources Defense Council. Table of U.S. Strategic Offensive Force Loadings. Archive of Nuclear Data. http://www.nrdc.org/nuclear/nudb/datab1.asp.

[15] U.S. Department of State, Bureau of Verification, Compliance, and Implementation, *The Legacy of START and Related U.S. Policies*, Fact Sheet, Washington, DC, July 16, 2009, http://www.state.gov/t/avc/rls/126119 htm.

Figure 2. U.S. Strategic Nuclear Forces: 1991-2014

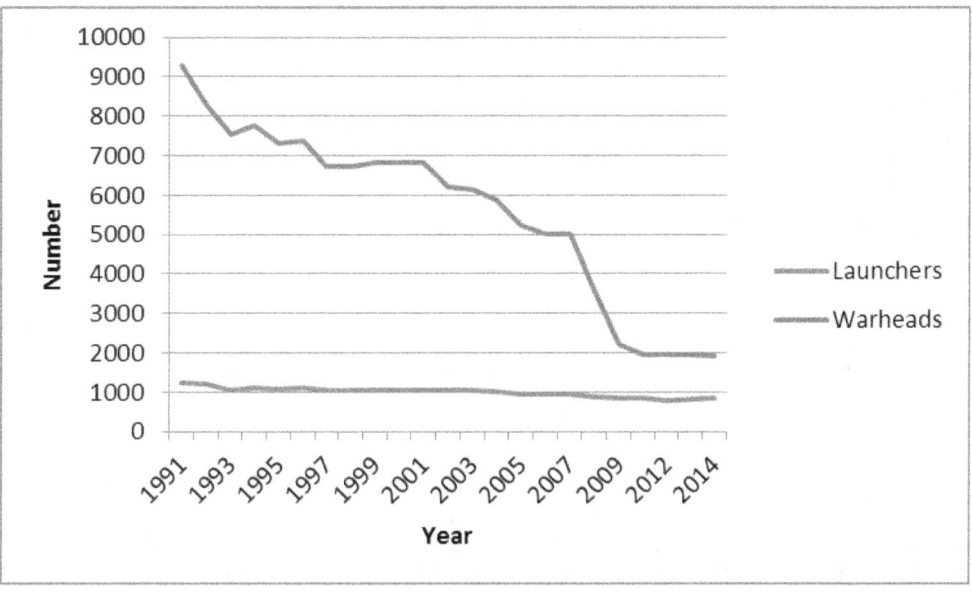

Source: Natural Resources Defense Council, Archive of Nuclear Data, Bulletin of Atomic Scientists, Nuclear Notebook.

During the 1990s, the United States continued to add to its Trident fleet, reaching a total of 18 submarines. It retired all of its remaining Poseidon submarines and all of the single-warhead Minuteman II missiles. It continued to deploy B-2 bombers, reaching a total of 21, and removed some of the older B-52G bombers from the nuclear fleet. Consequently, in 2001, its warheads were deployed on 18 Trident submarines with 24 missiles on each submarine and 6 or 8 warheads on each missile; 500 Minuteman III ICBMs, with up to 3 warheads on each missile; 50 Peacekeeper (MX) missiles, with 10 warheads on each missile; 94 B-52H bombers, with up to 20 cruise missiles on each bomber; and 21 B-2 bombers with up to 16 bombs on each aircraft.

The United States and Russia signed a second START Treaty in early 1993. Under this treaty, the United States would have had to reduce its strategic offensive nuclear weapons to between 3,000 and 3,500 accountable warheads. In 1994, the Department of Defense decided that, to meet this limit, it would deploy a force of 500 Minuteman III ICBMs with 1 warhead on each missile, 14 Trident submarines with 24 missiles on each submarine and 5 warheads on each missile, 76 B-52 bombers, and 21 B-2 bombers. The Air Force was to eliminate 50 Peacekeeper ICBMs and reorient the B-1 bombers to non-nuclear missions; the Navy would retire 4 Trident submarines (it later decided to convert these submarines to carry conventional weapons).

The START II Treaty never entered into force, and Congress prevented the Clinton Administration from reducing U.S. forces unilaterally to START II limits. Nevertheless, the Navy and Air Force continued to plan for the forces described above, and eventually implemented those changes. **Table 1** displays the forces the United States had deployed in 2001, after completing the START I reductions. It also includes those that it would have deployed under START II, in accordance with the 1994 decisions.

Table 1. U.S. Strategic Nuclear Forces Under START I and START II

System	Deployed under START I (2001)		Planned for START II	
	Launchers	Accountable Warheads[a]	Launchers	Accountable Warheads
Minuteman III ICBMs	500	1,200	500	500
Peacekeeper ICBMs	50	500	0	0
Trident I Missiles	168	1,008	0	0
Trident II Missiles	264	2,112	336	1,680
B-52 H Bombers (ALCM)	97	970	76	940
B-52 H Bombers (non-ALCM)	47	47	0	0
B-1 Bombers[b]	90	90	0	0
B-2 Bombers	20	20	21	336
Total	**1,237**	**5,948**	**933**	**3,456**

a. Under START I, bombers that are not equipped to carry ALCMs count as one warhead, even if they can carry up 16 nuclear bombs; bombers that are equipped to carry ALCMs count as 10 warheads, even if they can carry up to 20 ALCMs.

b. Although they still counted under START I, B-1 bombers are no longer equipped for nuclear missions.

The George W. Bush Administration stated in late 2001 that the United States would reduce its strategic nuclear forces to 1,700-2,200 "operationally deployed warheads" over the next decade.[16] This goal was codified in the 2002 Moscow Treaty. According to the Bush Administration, operationally deployed warheads were those deployed on missiles and stored near bombers on a day-to-day basis. They are the warheads that would be available immediately, or in a matter of days, to meet "immediate and unexpected contingencies."[17] The Administration also indicated that the United States would retain a triad of ICBMs, SLBMs, and heavy bombers for the foreseeable future. It did not, however, offer a rationale for this traditional "triad," although the points raised in the past about the differing and complementary capabilities of the systems probably still pertain. Admiral James Ellis, the former Commander of the U.S. Strategic Command (STRATCOM), highlighted this when he noted in a 2005 interview that the ICBM force provides responsiveness, the SLBM force provides survivability, and bombers provide flexibility and recall capability.[18]

The Bush Administration did not specify how it would reduce the U.S. arsenal from around 6,000 warheads to the lower level of 2,200 operationally deployed warheads, although it did identify some force structure changes that would account for part of the reductions. Specifically, after Congress removed its restrictions,[19] the United States eliminated the 50 Peacekeeper ICBMs,

---

[16] President Bush announced the U.S. intention to reduce its forces on November 13, 2001, during a summit with Russia's President Vladimir Putin. The United States and Russia codified these reductions in a Treaty signed in May 2002. See CRS Report RL31448, *Nuclear Arms Control: The Strategic Offensive Reductions Treaty*, by Amy F. Woolf.

[17] U.S. Senate. Committee on Armed Services. Statement of the Honorable Douglas J. Feith, Undersecretary of Defense For Policy. February 14, 2002.

[18] Hebert, Adam. The Future Missile Force. *Air Force Magazine*. October 2005.

[19] Beginning in FY1996, and continuing through the end of the Clinton Administration, Congress had prohibited the use of any DOD funds for the elimination of strategic nuclear delivery vehicles, below START I levels, until START II entered into force. See, for example, the FY1998 Defense Authorization Act (P.L. 105-85, §1302). Congress lifted this (continued...)

reducing by 500 the total number of operationally deployed ICBM warheads. It also continued with plans to remove four Trident submarines from service, and converted those ships to carry non-nuclear guided missiles. These submarines would have counted as 476 warheads under the START Treaty's rules. These changes reduced U.S. forces to around 5,000 warheads on 950 delivery vehicles in 2006; this reduction appears in **Figure 2**. The Bush Administration also noted that two of the Trident submarines remaining in the fleet would be in overhaul at any given time. The warheads that could be carried on those submarines would not count against the Moscow Treaty limits because they would not be "operationally deployed." This would further reduce the U.S. deployed force by 200 to 400 warheads.

The Bush Administration, through the 2005 Strategic Capabilities Assessment and 2006 Quadrennial Defense Review, announced additional changes in U.S. ICBMs, SLBMs, and bomber forces; these included the elimination of 50 Minuteman III missiles and several hundred air-launched cruise missiles. (These are discussed in more detail below.) These changes appeared to be sufficient to reduce the number of operationally deployed warheads enough to meet the treaty limit of 2,200 warheads, as the United States announced, in mid-2009, that it had met this limit. Reaching this level, however, also depends on the number of warheads carried by each of the remaining Trident and Minuteman missiles.[20]

Current and Future Force Structure and Size

The Obama Administration indicated in the 2010 NPR that the United States will retain a triad of ICBMs, SLBMs, and heavy bombers as the United States reduces its forces to the limits in the 2010 New START Treaty. The NPR indicated that the unique characteristics of each leg of the triad were important to the goal of maintaining strategic stability at reduced numbers of warheads:

> Each leg of the Triad has advantages that warrant retaining all three legs at this stage of reductions. Strategic nuclear submarines (SSBNs) and the SLBMs they carry represent the most survivable leg of the U.S. nuclear Triad.... Single-warhead ICBMs contribute to stability, and like SLBMs are not vulnerable to air defenses. Unlike ICBMs and SLBMs, bombers can be visibly deployed forward, as a signal in crisis to strengthen deterrence of potential adversaries and assurance of allies and partners.[21]

Moreover, the NPR noted that "retaining sufficient force structure in each leg to allow the ability to hedge effectively by shifting weight from one Triad leg to another if necessary due to unexpected technological problems or operational vulnerabilities."[22]

The Administration continues to support the triad, even as reduces U.S. nuclear forces under New START and considers whether to reduce U.S. nuclear forces further in the coming years. In April 2013, Madelyn Creedon, the Assistant Secretary of Defense for Global Security Affairs, stated,

---

(...continued)

restriction in the FY2002 Defense Authorization Act (P.L. 107-107, §1031).

[20] "U.S. Meets Moscow Nuclear Reduction Commitment Three Years Early," *Global Security Newswire*, February 11, 2009.

[21] U.S. Department of Defense, *Nuclear Posture Review*, Washington, DC, April 6, 2010, p. 22. http://www.defense.gov/npr/docs/2010%20Nuclear%20Posture%20Review%20Report.pdf.

[22] Ibid., p. 20.

"The 2010 nuclear posture review concluded that the United States will maintain a triad of ICBMs, SLBMs, and nuclear capable heavy bombers. And the president's F.Y. '14 budget request supports modernization of these nuclear forces."[23] Further, in its report on the Nuclear Employment Strategy of the United States, released in June 2013, DOD states that the United States will maintain a nuclear triad, because this is the best way to "maintain strategic stability at reasonable cost, while hedging against potential technical problems or vulnerabilities."[24]

On April 8, 2014, the Obama Administration released a report detailing the force structure that the United States would deploy under New START.[25] It indicated that, although the reductions would be complete by the treaty deadline of February 5, 2018, most of the reductions would come late in the treaty implementation period so that the plans could change, if necessary. **Table 2** displays this force structure and compares it with estimates of U.S. operational strategic nuclear forces in 2010. This force structure is consistent with the statements and adjustments the Administration has made about deploying all Minuteman III missiles with a single warhead, retaining Trident submarines deployed in two oceans, and converting some number of heavy bombers to conventional-only missions.

Table 2. U.S. Strategic Nuclear Forces under New START

(Estimated Current Forces and Potential New START Forces)

	Estimated Forces, 2010		Possible Forces Under New START, 2018[a]		
	Launchers	Warheads	Total Launchers	Deployed Launchers	Warheads
Minuteman III	450	500	454	400	400
Trident	336	1,152	280	240	1,090
B-52	76	300	46	42	42
B-2	18	200	20	18	18
Total	**880**	**2,152**	**800**	**700**	**1,550**

Source: U.S. Department of Defense, Report on Plan to Implement the Nuclear Force Reductions, Limitations, and Verification, Washington, DC, April 8, 2014.

a. Under this force the United States will retain 14 Trident submarines with 2 in overhaul. In accordance with the terms of New START, the United States will eliminate 4 launchers on each submarine, so that each counts as only 20 launchers. The United States will also retain all 450 Minuteman III launchers, although only 400 would hold deployed missiles.

---

[23] U.S. Congress, House Armed Forces, Strategic Forces, Hearing on the Proposed Fiscal 2014 Defense Authorization as it Relates to Atomic Energy Defense Activities, 113th Cong., 1st sess., May 9, 2013.

[24] U.S. Department of Defense, *Report on Nuclear Employment Strategy of the United States*, Washington, DC, June 2013, p. 5, http://www.defense.gov/pubs/reporttoCongressonUSNuclearEmploymentStrategy_Section491.pdf.

[25] U.S. Department of Defense, *Report on Plan to Implement the Nuclear Force Reductions, Limitations, and Verification*, Washington, DC, April 8, 2014, http://www.defense.gov/documents/New-START-Implementation-Report.pdf.

Strategic Nuclear Delivery Vehicles: Recent Reductions and Current Modernization Programs

Intercontinental Ballistic Missiles (ICBMs)

Peacekeeper (MX)

In the late 1980s, the United States deployed 50 Peacekeeper ICBMs, each with 10 warheads, at silos that had held Minuteman missiles at F.E. Warren Air Force Base in Wyoming. The 1993 START II Treaty would have banned multiple warhead ICBMs, so the United States would have had to eliminate these missiles while implementing the treaty. Therefore, the Pentagon began planning for their elimination, and the Air Force added funds to its budget for this purpose in 1994. However, beginning in FY1998, Congress prohibited the Clinton Administration from spending any money on the deactivation or retirement of these missiles until START II entered into force. The Bush Administration requested $14 million in FY2002 to begin the missiles' retirement; Congress lifted the restriction and authorized the funding. The Air Force began to deactivate the missiles in October 2002, and completed the process, having removed all the missiles from their silos, in September 2005. The MK21 reentry vehicles and W87 warheads from these missiles have been placed in storage. As is noted below, the Air Force plans to redeploy some of these warheads and reentry vehicles on Minuteman III missiles, under the Safety Enhanced Reentry Vehicle (SERV) program.

Under the terms of the original, 1991 START Treaty, the United States would have had to eliminate the Peacekeeper missile silos to remove the warheads on the missiles from accountability under the treaty limits. However, the Air Force retained the silos as it deactivated the missiles. Therefore, the warheads that were deployed on the Peacekeeper missiles still counted under START, even though the missiles were no longer operational, until START expired in December 2009. The United States did not, however, count any of these warheads under the limits in the Moscow Treaty. They also will not count under the limits in the New START Treaty, if the United States eliminates the silos. It will not, however, have to blow up or excavate the silos, as it would have had to do under the original START Treaty. The new START Treaty indicates that the parties can use whatever method they choose to eliminate the silos, as long as they demonstrate that the silos can no longer launch missiles. The Air Force plans to fill the silos with gravel to eliminate them, with this process beginning in 2015.

Minuteman III

The U.S. Minuteman III ICBMs are located at three Air Force bases—F.E. Warren AFB in Wyoming, Malmstrom AFB in Montana, and Minot AFB in North Dakota. Each base houses 150 missiles.

Force Structure Changes

In the 2006 Quadrennial Defense Review (QDR), the Pentagon indicated that it planned to "reduce the number of deployed Minuteman III ballistic missiles from 500 to 450, beginning in Fiscal Year 2007."[26] The Air Force deactivated the missiles in Malmstrom's 564th Missile Squadron, which was known as the "odd squad."[27] This designation reflected that the launch control facilities for these missiles were built and installed by General Electric, while all other Minuteman launch control facilities were built by Boeing; as a result, these missiles used a different communications and launch control system than all the other Minuteman missiles. According to Air Force Space Command, the drawdown began on July 1, 2007. All of the reentry vehicles were removed from the missiles in early 2008, the missiles were all removed from their silos by the end of July 2008, and the squadron was deactivated by the end of August 2008.[28]

In testimony before the Senate Armed Services Committee, General Cartwright stated that the Air Force had decided to retire these missiles so that they could serve as test assets for the remaining force. He noted that the Air Force had to "keep a robust test program all the way through the life of the program."[29] With the test assets available before this decision, the test program would begin to run short around 2017 or 2018. The added test assets would support the program through 2025 or longer. This time line, however, raises questions about why the Air Force pressed to begin retiring the missiles in FY2007, 10 years before it would run out of test assets. Some have speculated that the elimination of the 50 missiles was intended to reduce the long-term operations and maintenance costs for the fleet, particularly since the 564th Squadron used different ground control technologies and training systems than the remainder of the fleet. This option was not likely, however, to produce budgetary savings in the near term as the added cost of deactivating the missiles could exceed the reductions in operations and maintenance expenses.[30] In addition, to use these missiles as test assets, the Air Force has had to include them in the modernization programs described below. This has further limited the budgetary savings.

When the Air Force decided to retire 50 ICBMs at Malmstrom, it indicated that it would retain the silos and would not destroy or eliminate them. However, with the signing of the New START Treaty in 2010, these silos added to the U.S. total of nondeployed ICBM launchers. So the Air Force now plans to eliminate them, by filling them with gravel in 2014, so that the United States can comply with the New START limits by 2018.

In a pattern that has become common over the years, Congress questioned the Administration's rationale for the plan to retire 50 Minuteman missiles, indicating that it believed that more Minuteman silos increased U.S. security and strengthened deterrence. In the FY2007 Defense Authorization Act (H.R. 5122, §139), Congress stated that DOD could not spend any money to begin the withdrawal of these missiles from the active force until the Secretary of Defense submitted a report that addressed a number of issues, including (1) a detailed justification for the proposal to reduce the force from 500 to 450 missiles; (2) a detailed analysis of the strategic ramifications of continuing to equip a portion of the force with multiple independent warheads

---

[26] U.S. Department of Defense. Report of the 2006 Quadrennial Defense Review. Washington, February 2006. p. 50.

[27] Johnson, Peter. Growth Worries Base Boosters. *Great Falls Tribune*. January 19, 2006.

[28] Global Security Newswire. U.S. Deactivates 50 Strategic Missiles. August 4, 2008.

[29] U.S. Senate, Committee on Armed Services, Hearing on Global Strike Plans and Programs. Testimony of James E. Cartwright, Commander U.S. Strategic Command. March 29, 2006.

[30] Private communication.

rather than single warheads; (3) an assessment of the test assets and spares required to maintain a force of 500 missiles and a force of 450 missiles through 2030; (4) an assessment of whether halting upgrades to the missiles withdrawn from the deployed force would compromise their ability to serve as test assets; and (5) a description of the plan for extending the life of the Minuteman III missile force beyond FY2030. The Secretary of Defense submitted this report to Congress in late March 2007.

Although the retirement of 50 Minuteman III missiles probably did little to reduce the cost of maintaining and operating the Minuteman fleet, this program did allow both STRATCOM and the Air Force to participate in the effort to transform the Pentagon in response to post-Cold War threats. These missiles may still have a role to play in U.S. national security strategy, but they may not be needed in the numbers that were required when the United States faced the Soviet threat.

In the April 2014 report on its planned force structure under New START, the Obama Administration indicated that it plans to retain 400 deployed Minuteman III ICBMs, within a total force of 450 deployed and nondeployed launchers. According to Air Force officials, this option is attractive because it would allow the Air Force to deactivate missiles in silos that have been damaged by water intrusion, repair those silos, and possibly return missiles to them at a later date while it repaired additional silos. If it had eliminated some of the empty silos, it would have had to do so in complete squadrons, regardless of the silos' conditions, and would not have been able to empty and repair the most degraded silos.[31] Congress has also weighed in on this force structure, again arguing that U.S. security would benefit from the retention of more operational ICBM launchers, even if they did not contain operational missiles.

During 2012 and 2013, Congress sought to prevent the Administration from initiating an environmental assessment that would advise the possible elimination of up to 50 silos under New START. In addition, the House Armed Services Committee included a provision in its version of the FY2015 National Defense Authorization Act (H.R. 4435, Sec. 1634) that would require the Air Force to retain all 450 ICBM silos, regardless of future force structure requirements, budgets, or arms control limits, through 2015. The provision states that "it is in the national security interests of the United States to retain the maximum number of land-based strategic missile silos and their associated infrastructure to ensure that billions of dollars in prior taxpayer investments for such silos and infrastructure are not lost through precipitous actions which may be budget-driven, cyclical, and not in the long-term strategic interests of the United States." It requires that the Secretary of Defense "preserve each intercontinental ballistic missile silo ... in warm status that enables such silo to—(1) remain a fully functioning element of the interconnected and redundant command and control system of the missile field; and (2) be made fully operational with a deployed missile."

Warhead Plans

Each Minuteman III missile was initially deployed with 3 warheads, for a total of 1,500 warheads across the force. In 2001, to meet the START limit of 6,000 warheads, the United States removed 2 warheads from each of the 150 Minuteman missiles at F.E. Warren AFB,[32] reducing the

---

[31] Gabe Starosta, "On New START, Timing Begins to Limit Force-Structure Alternatives," *InsideDefense.com*, May 14, 2013.

[32] See Robert S. Norris and Hans M. Kristensen. U.S. Nuclear Forces, 2006. Bulletin of the Atomic Scientists. (continued...)

Minuteman III force to 1,200 total warheads. In the process, the Air Force also removed and destroyed the "bulkhead," the platform on the reentry vehicle, so that, in accordance with START rules, these missiles can no longer carry three warheads.

Under START II, the United States would have had to download all the Minuteman III missiles to one warhead each. Although the Bush Administration initially endorsed the plan to download all Minuteman ICBMs, this plan apparently changed. In an interview with *Air Force Magazine* in October 2003, General Robert Smolen indicated that the Air Force would maintain the ability to deploy these 500 missiles with up to 800 warheads.[33] Although some analysts interpreted this statement to mean that the Minuteman ICBMs would carry 800 warheads on a day-to-day basis, it seems more likely that this was a reference to the Air Force intent to maintain the ability to reload warheads, and reconstitute the force, if circumstances changed.[34] The 2001 NPR had indicated that the United States would maintain the flexibility to do this. However, in testimony before the Senate Armed Services Committee, General Cartwright also indicated that some Minuteman missiles might carry more than one warhead. Specifically, when discussing the reduction from 500 to 450 missiles, he said, "this is not a reduction in the number of warheads deployed. They will just merely be re-distributed on the missiles."[35] Major General Deppe confirmed that the Air Force would retain some Minuteman III missiles with more than one warhead when he noted, in a speech in mid-April 2007, that the remaining 450 Minuteman III missiles could be deployed with one, two, or three warheads.[36]

In the 2010 NPR, the Obama Administration indicated that, under the New START Treaty, all of the U.S. Minuteman III missiles will carry only one warhead. It indicated that this configuration would "enhance the stability of the nuclear balance by reducing incentives for either side to strike first."[37] The Air Force completed the downloading process, leaving all Minuteman III missiles with a single warhead, on June 16, 2014.[38] Unlike under START, the United States did not have to alter the front end of the missile or remove the old bulkhead. As a result, the United States could restore warheads to its ICBM force if the international security environment changed. Moreover, this plan could have changed, if, in an effort to reduce the cost of the ICBM force under New START, the Administration had decided to reduce the number of Minuteman III missiles further in the coming years. Reports indicate that the Pentagon may have reviewed such an option as a part of its NPR implementation study, but, as the report released on April 8, 2014, indicated, it did not decide to pursue this approach. As a result, under New START, each of the 400 deployed Minuteman III missiles will carry a single warhead.

(...continued)

January/February 2006.

[33] Hebert, Adam. The Future Missile Force. *Air Force Magazine*. October 2005.

[34] See, for example, Jeffrey Lewis. STRATCOM Hearts MIRV. ArmsControlWonk.com, January 30, 2006.

[35] See, U.S. Senate, Committee on Armed Services, Hearing on Global Strike Plans and Programs. Testimony of James E. Cartwright, Commander U.S. Strategic Command. March 29, 2006.

[36] Sirak, Michael. Air Force Prepared To Draaw Down Minuteman III Fleet by 50 Missiles. Defense Daily. April 17, 2007.

[37] Single-warhead ICBMs are considered to be stabilizing because it would take two attacking warheads to destroy the silo. If each side has approximately the same number of warheads, than an attack on a single warhead missile would cost more warheads than it would kill, and, therefore, would not be considered to be lucrative.

[38] Jenn Rowell, "Last Malmstron ICBM Reconfigured Under Treaty," *Great Falls Tribune*, June 18, 2014.

Minuteman Modernization Programs

The Air Force has pursued several programs that are designed to improve the accuracy and reliability of the Minuteman fleet and to extend the missiles' service lives. According to some estimates, this effort could eventually cost $6 billion-$7 billion.[39] This section describes several of the key programs in this effort.

Propulsion Replacement Program (PRP)

The program began in 1998 and has been replacing the propellant, the solid rocket fuel, in the Minuteman motors to extend the life of the rocket motors. A consortium led by Northrup Grumman poured the new fuel into the first and second stages and remanufactured the third stages of the missiles. According to the Air Force, as of early August, 2007, 325 missiles, or 72% of the fleet, had completed the PRP program; this number increased to around 80% by mid-2008. The Air Force purchased the final 56 booster sets, for a total of 601, with its funding in FY2008. Funding in FY2009 supported the assembly of the remaining boosters. The Air Force expects to complete the PRP program by 2013.[40] In the FY2007 Defense Authorization Act (P.L. 109-364) and the FY2007 Defense Appropriations Act (P.L. 109-289), the 109th Congress indicated that it would not support efforts to end this program early. However, in its budget request for FY2010, the Air Force indicated that FY2009 was the last year for funding for the program.

Guidance Replacement Program (GRP)

The Guidance Replacement Program has extended the service life of the Minuteman missiles' guidance set, and improved the maintainability and reliability of guidance sets. It replaced aging parts with more modern and reliable technologies, while maintaining the accuracy of the missiles.[41] Flight testing for the new system began in 1998, and, at the time, it exceeded its operational requirements. Production began in 2000, and the Air Force purchased 652 of the new guidance units. Press reports indicate that the system had some problems with accuracy during its testing program.[42] The Air Force eventually identified and corrected the problems in 2002 and 2003. According to the Air Force, 425 Minuteman III missiles were upgraded with the new guidance packages as of early August 2007. The Air Force had been taking delivery of 5 to7 new guidance units each month, for a total of 652 units. Boeing reported that it had delivered the final guidance set in early February 2009. The Air Force did not request any additional funding for this program in FY2010. However, it did request $1.2 million in FY2011 and $0.6 million in FY2012 to complete the program.

---

[39] Robert S. Norris and Hans M. Kristensen. U.S. Nuclear Forces, 2006. Bulletin of the Atomic Scientists. January/February 2006.

[40] Sirak, Michael. Minuteman Fleet has Life Beyond 2020, Says Senior Air Force Space Official. Defense Daily. June 14, 2006.

[41] LGM Minuteman III Modernization. Globalsecurity.org.

[42] Donnelly, John M. Air Force Defends Spending Half A Billion on Iffy ICBMs. *Defense Week.* September 10, 2001. p. 1.

Propulsion System Rocket Engine Program (PSRE)

According to the Air Force, the Propulsion System Rocket Engine (PSRE) program is designed to rebuild and replace Minuteman post-boost propulsion system components that were produced in the 1970s. The Air Force has been replacing, rather than repairing this system because original replacement parts, materials, and components are no longer available. This program is designed to reduce the life-cycle costs of the Minuteman missiles and maintain their reliability through 2020. The Air Force plans to purchase a total of 574 units for this program. Through FY2009, the Air Force had purchased 441 units, at a cost of $128 million. It requested an additional $26.2 million to purchase another 96 units in FY2010 and $21.5 million to purchase 37 units in FY2011. This would complete the purchase of the units. As a result, the budget for FY2012 does not support the purchase of any additional units, but does include $26.1 million for continuing work installing the units. The FY2013 budget request contained $10.8 million for the same purpose.

Rapid Execution and Combat Targeting (REACT) Service Life Extension Program

The REACT targeting system was first installed in Minuteman launch control centers in the mid-1990s. This technology allowed for a significant reduction in the amount of time it would take to retarget the missiles, automated routine functions to reduce the workload for the crews, and replaced obsolete equipment.[43] In 2006, the Air Force began to deploy a modernized version of this system to extend its service life and to update the command and control capability of the launch control centers. This program will allow for more rapid retargeting of ICBMs, a capability identified in the Nuclear Posture Review as essential to the future nuclear force. The Air Force completed this effort in late 2006.

Safety Enhanced Reentry Vehicle (SERV)

As was noted above, under the SERV program, the Air Force plans to deploy MK21/W-87 reentry vehicles removed from Peacekeeper ICBMs on the Minuteman missiles, replacing the older MK12/W62 and MK12A/W78 reentry vehicles. To do this, the Air Force must modify the software, change the mounting on the missile, and change the support equipment. According to Air Force Space Command, the SERV program conducted three flight tests in 2005 and cancelled a fourth test because the first three were so successful.[44] The Air Force installed 20 of the kits for the new reentry vehicles on the Minuteman missiles at F.E. Warren Air Force Base in 2006. The process began at Malmstrom in July 2007 and at Minot in July 2008. As of early August 2007, 47 missiles had been modified. The Air Force purchase an additional 111 modification kits in FY2009, for a total of 570 kits. This was the last year that it planned to request funding for the program. It planned to complete the installation process by 2012.

This program will likely ensure the reliability and effectiveness of the Minuteman III missiles throughout their planned deployments. The W-87 warheads entered the U.S. arsenal in 1986 and were refurbished in 2005. This process extended their service life past 2025.[45]

---

[43] LGM Minuteman III Modernization. Globalsecurity.org.

[44] Lt. Gen. Frank G. Klotz, Vice Commander, Air Force Space Command. Transcript of Speech to the National Defense University Breakfast. June 13, 2006.

[45] Tom Collina, *Fact Sheet: U.S. Nuclear Modernization*, Arms Control Association, Washington, DC, January 5, 2009, (continued...)

Solid Rocket Motor Warm Line Program

In the FY2009 Omnibus Appropriations Bill, Congress approved a new program known as the Solid Rocket Motor Warm Line Program. According to Air Force budget documents, this program is intended to "sustain and maintain the unique manufacturing and engineering infrastructure necessary to preserve the Minuteman III solid rocket motor production capability" by providing funding to maintain a low rate of production of motors each year.[46] The program received $42.9 million in FY2010 and produced motors for four Minuteman ICBMs. DOD requested $44.2 million to produce motors for three additional ICBMs in FY2011. The budget request for FY2012 includes an additional $34 million to complete work on the motors purchased in prior years. The FY2013 budget did not contain any additional funding for this program area.

ICBM Dem/Val Program

The Air Force is also funding, through its RDT&E budget, a number of programs under the ICBM Dem/Val (demonstration and validation) title that will allow it to mature technologies that it might use in a future ICBM program. These programs might also provide support to efforts to maintain the current ICBM system through 2030. Congress appropriated $71.8 million for this program area in FY2012 and FY2013 and $73 million in FY2014. The Administration has requested an additional $30.9 million for FY2014. Press reports indicate that the decline in funding in this program area could delay some technologies needed for the future ICBM program. Specifically, Air Force officials have indicated that work on a new solid-state guidance system could be delayed by two to three years.[47] This new system would increase the accuracy of the ICBM force and allow the missiles to destroy hardened targets with a single warhead.

Future Programs

In 2002, the Air Force began to explore its options for a new missile to replace the Minuteman III, with the intent to begin deploying a new missile in 2018. It reportedly produced a "mission needs statement" at that time, and then began an Analysis of Alternatives (AOA) in 2004.[48] In June 2006, General Frank Klotz indicated that, after completing the AOA, Air Force Space Command had decided to recommend "an evolutionary approach to the replacement of the Minuteman III capability,"[49] which would continue to modernize the components of the existing missiles rather than begin from scratch to develop and produce new missiles. He indicated that Space Command supported this approach because it would be less costly than designing a new system "from scratch."

(...continued)

http://www.armscontrol.org/USNuclearModernization.

[46] http://www.saffm hq.af mil/shared/media/document/AFD-100128-067.pdf.

[47] Elaine Grossman, "Key Targeting Tech for Future U.S. Nuclear Missile has Gone Unfunded," *Nextgov.com*, August 19, 2014.

[48] Selinger, Mark. Minuteman Replacement Study Expected to Begin Soon. Aerospace Daily and Defense Report. June 25, 2004.

[49] Lt. Gen. Frank G. Klotz, Vice Commander, Air Force Space Command. Transcript of Speech to the National Defense University Breakfast. June 13, 2006.

With this plan in place, the Air Force began examining the investments that might be needed to sustain the Minuteman force through 2030. According to General Robert Kehler, then Commander-in-Chief of STRATCOM, the missile should be viable throughout that time.[50] In addition, according to DOD officials, flight tests and surveillance programs undertaken over the next few years should provide the Air Force with "better estimates for component age-out and system end-of-life timelines."[51]

At the same time, the Air Force has begun to consider what a follow-on system to the Minuteman III might look like for the time frame after 2030. The Air Force began a capabilities-based assessment of its land-based deterrent in early 2011 and began a new Analysis of Alternatives (AOA) for the ICBM force in 2012 with completion expected in mid-2014.[52] According to the Air Force, it requested $2.6 million to begin the study in the FY2012 budget and it plans to spend $26 million between FY2012 and FY2014. The FY2013 budget request includes $11.7 million for a new project area known as Ground-based Strategic Deterrence (GBSD). According to the Air Force, this effort, which was previously funded under Long-Range Planning, includes funding to begin the Analysis of Alternatives (AOA). The FY2014 budget request included $9.4 million to continue this study.

In early January 2013, the Air Force Nuclear Weapons Center issued a "Broad Agency Announcement (BAA)" seeking white papers for concepts "that address modernization or replacement of the ground-based leg of the nuclear triad." The papers produced as a part of this study will represent an early evaluation of alternatives for the future of the ICBM force, and may help select those concepts that will be included in the formal Analysis of Alternatives. According to the BAA, the Air Force Nuclear Weapons Center created five possible paths for further analysis. These include one that would continue to use the current Minuteman III baseline until 2075 without seeking to close gaps in the missiles' capabilities, one that would incorporate incremental changes into the current Minuteman III system to close gaps in capabilities, one that would design a new, fixed ICBM system to replace the Minuteman III, one that would design a new mobile ICBM system, and one that would design a new tunnel-based system.

Some analysts have expressed surprise at the possibility that the Air Force may consider deploying a new ICBM on mobile launchers or in tunnels. During the Cold War, the Air Force considered these types of deployment concepts as a way to increase the survivability of the ICBM force when faced with possibility of an attack with hundreds, or thousands, of Soviet warheads. Even during the Cold War, these concepts proved to be very expensive and impractical, and they were dropped from consideration after the demise of the Soviet Union and in the face of deep reductions in the numbers of U.S. and Russian warheads. Some analysts see the Air Force's possible renewed interest in these concepts as a step backward; they argue that the United States should consider retiring its ICBM force, and should not consider new, expensive schemes to increase the missiles' capabilities. Others, however, note that the presence of these concepts in the

---

[50] Jason Simpson, "Kehler: Air Force Investigating Minuteman III Follow-On System," *Inside the Air Force*, October 8, 2009. See, also, Jason Simpson, "Testers See no Problems With Minuteman III Missiles Lasting to 2030," *Inside the Air Force*, September 4, 2009.

[51] See the prepared statement of Assistant Secretary of Defense Madelyn Creedon, U.S. Congress, House Armed Forces, Strategic Forces, Hearing on the Proposed Fiscal 2014 Defense Authorization as it Relates to Atomic Energy Defense Activities. 113th Cong., 1st sess., May 9. 2013.

[52] U.S. Department of Defense, *November 2010 Update to the National Defense Authorization Act of FY2010*, New START Treaty Framework and Nuclear Force Structure Plans, Washington, DC, November 17, 2010, p. 11. http://www.lasg.org/CMRR/Sect1251_update_17Nov2010.pdf.

study does not mean that the Air Force will move in this direction. They note that the 2010 NPR mentioned the possibility of mobile basing for ICBMs as a way to increase warning and decision time, so it should not be a surprise to see requests for further study. However, the cost and complexity of mobile ICBM basing may again eliminate these concepts from further consideration.

According to press reports, this AOA has been completed and was briefed to industry officials in July 2014. The Air Force has reportedly decided to pursue a "hybrid" plan for the next generation ICBM. It would maintain the basic design of the missile, the current communications system, and the existing launch silos, but would replace the rocket motors and guidance sets. Reports also indicate that, although this missile would be deployed in fixed silos, the design would allow the missiles to be deployed on mobile launchers sometime in the future.[53]

While the Air Force appears committed to pursuing the replacement of Minuteman III missile with a new system, there is growing recognition among analysts that fiscal constraints may alter this approach. As is noted below, all three legs of the U.S. nuclear triad are currently slated for modernization in the next 10 to 20 years. Each of these programs is likely to stress the budgets and financial capabilities of the services. Nevertheless, the Air Force has sought to allocate more funds to its nuclear missions, both to address personnel and operational issues that have come up in recent years and to pursue its modernization programs. According to the Secretary of the Air Force, Deborah Lee James, the nuclear capabilities of the Air Force are a national asset, so added funding could come not only from the Air Force budget but also from the broader Pentagon budget.[54]

Submarine Launched Ballistic Missiles

The U.S. fleet of ballistic missile submarines consists of 14 Trident (Ohio-class) submarines, each equipped to carry 24 Trident missiles. With 2 submarines in overhaul, the operational fleet of 12 submarines currently carries around 1,100 warheads. Under the New START Treaty, each of the submarines will be modified so that they can carry only 20 missiles. The four empty launch tubes will be modified so that they cannot launch missiles; this will remove them from accountability under New START. As a result, the 14 submarines will count as a total of 280 deployed and nondeployed launchers, with 240 deployed launchers counting on the 12 operational submarines. The Navy plans to begin the process of reducing the number of launchers on each submarine in FY2015.

By the early 1990s, the United States had completed the deployment of 18 Trident ballistic missile submarines (SSBNs). Each of these submarines was equipped to carry 24 Trident missiles, and each missile could carry up to 8 warheads (either W-76 warheads or the larger W-88 warheads on the Trident II missile). The Navy initially deployed eight of these submarines at Bangor, WA, and all eight were equipped with the older Trident I missile. It then deployed 10 submarines, all equipped with the Trident II missile, at Kings Bay, GA. During the 1994 Nuclear Posture Review, the Clinton Administration decided that the United States would reduce the size

---

[53] Elaine Grossman, "Key Targeting Tech for Future U.S. Nuclear Missile has Gone Unfunded," *Nextgov.com*, August 19, 2014.

[54] James Drew, "Air Force Wants OSD to Allocate More Funds for Nuclear Enterprise," *Inside the Air Force*, August 1, 2014.

of its Trident fleet to 14 submarines, and that 4 of the older submarines would be "backfit" to carry the Trident II missile.

The Bush Administration's 2001 Nuclear Posture Review endorsed the plan to backfit four of the Trident submarines so that all would carry Trident II missiles. It also indicated that, instead of retiring the remaining four submarines, the Navy would convert them to carry conventional weapons, and designated them "guided missile" submarines (SSGNs). The 2010 NPR also endorsed a force of 14 Trident submarines, although it noted that it might reduce that force to 12 submarines in the latter half of this decade. As was noted above, each submarine will deploy with only 20 missiles to meet the reductions in New START. As a result, the U.S. ballistic missile submarine (SSBN) force may continue to consist of 14 Trident submarines, with 2 in overhaul, through New START implementation.

The SSGN Program

The Navy converted four Trident submarines (the *USS Ohio, USS Michigan, USS Florida*, and *USS Georgia*) to carry conventional cruise missiles and other conventional weapons. Reports indicate that the conversion process took approximately $1 billion and two years for each of the four submarines. The SSGNs can each carry 154 Tomahawk cruise missiles, along with up to 100 special forces troops and their mini-submarines.[55]

The first two submarines scheduled for this conversion were removed from the nuclear fleet in early 2003. They were slated to receive their engineering overhaul, then to begin the conversion process in 2004.[56] The first to complete the process, the *USS Ohio* returned to service as an SSGN in January 2006[57] and achieved operational status on November 1, 2007. According to the Navy, the *Georgia* was scheduled for deployment in March 2008, and the other submarines were scheduled to reach that status later in the year.[58] According to Admiral Stephen Johnson, the Director of the Navy's Strategic Submarine Program (SSP), all four of the submarines had returned to service by mid-2008, and two were forward-deployed on routine patrols. They are likely to remain in service through the mid-2020s.

The Backfit Program

As was noted above, both the 1994 and 2001 Nuclear Posture Reviews confirmed that the Navy would backfit four Trident submarines so that they could carry the newer Trident II (D-5) missile. This process not only allowed the Navy to replace the aging C-4 missiles, it also equipped the fleet with a missile that has improved accuracy and a larger payload. With its greater range, it would allow the submarines to operate in a larger area and cover a greater range of targets. These characteristics were valued when the system was designed and the United States sought to

---

[55]Connolly, Allison. For Four Subs, Its Good-bye Ballistic Missiles, Hello SEALs. Norfolk Virginia Pilot. December 18, 2004.

[56] Ohio Class SSGN Tactical Trident. GlobalSecurity.org http://www.globalsecurity.org/military/systems/ship/ssgn-726 htm.

[57] First Trident Submarine Converted. Associated Press. January 10, 2006.

[58] U.S. Congress. Senate. Armed Services Committee, Subcommittee on Strategic Forces. Fiscal Year 2008 Strategic Forces Program Budget. Hearing. Prepared statement of Mr. Brian R. Green, Deputy Assistant Secretary of Defense, Strategic Capabilities, p. 6. March 28, 2007. See also, Guided Missile Submarine Ohio Ready for Deployment. Inside the Navy, November 5, 2007.

enhance its ability to deter the Soviet Union. The Bush Administration believed that the range, payload, and flexibility of the Trident submarines and D-5 missiles remained relevant in an era when the United States may seek to deter or defeat a wider range of adversaries. The Obama Administration has emphasized that, by providing the United States with a secure second strike capability, these submarines enhance strategic stability.

Four of the eight Trident submarines based in Bangor, WA (*USS Alaska*, *USS Nevada*, *USS Henry M. Jackson*, and *USS Alabama*) were a part of the backfit program. The *Alaska* and *Nevada* both began the process in 2001; the *Alaska* completed its backfit and rejoined the fleet in March 2002 and the *Nevada* did the same in August 2002. During the process, the submarines underwent a pre-planned engineered refueling overhaul, which accomplishes a number of maintenance objectives, including refueling of the reactor, repairing and upgrading some equipment, replacing obsolete equipment, repairing or upgrading the ballistic missile systems, and other minor alterations.[59] The submarines also are fit with the Trident II missiles and the operating systems that are unique to these missiles. According to the Navy, both of these efforts came in ahead of schedule and under budget. The *Henry M. Jackson* and *Alabama* were completed their engineering overhaul and backfit in FY2006 and reentered the fleet in 2007 and 2008.

The last of the Trident I (C-4) missiles was removed from the fleet in October 2004, when the *USS Alabama* off-loaded its missiles and began the overhaul and backfit process. All the Trident submarines currently in the U.S. fleet now carry the Trident II missile.[60]

Basing Changes

When the Navy first decided, in the mid-1990s, to maintain a Trident fleet with 14 submarines, it planned to "balance" the fleet by deploying 7 Trident submarines at each of the 2 Trident bases. The Navy would have transferred three submarines from Kings Bay to Bangor, after four of the submarines from Bangor were removed from the ballistic missile fleet, for a balance of seven submarines at each base. However, these plans changed after the Bush Administration's Nuclear Posture Review. The Navy has transferred five submarines to Bangor, "balancing" the fleet by basing nine submarines at Bangor and five submarines at Kings Bay. Because two submarines would be in overhaul at any given time, this basing plan means that seven submarines would be operational at Bangor and five would be operational at Kings Bay.

According to unclassified reports, the Navy began moving Trident submarines from Kings Bay to Bangor in 2002, and transferred the fifth submarine in September 2005.[61] This change in basing pattern apparently reflects changes in the international security environment, with fewer targets within range of submarines operating in the Atlantic, and a greater number of targets within range of submarines operating in the Pacific. In particular, the shift allows the United States to improve its coverage of targets in China and North Korea.[62] Further, as the United States modifies its nuclear targeting objectives it could alter the patrol routes for the submarines operating in both

---

[59] SSBN-726 Ohio-Class FBM Submarines, GlobalSecurity.org, http://www.globalsecurity.org/wmd/systems/ssbn-726-recent htm.

[60] Morris, Jefferson. Older Trident Missiles to be Phased out by Fall, Admiral Says. Aerospace Daily and Defense Report, June 17, 2005.

[61] Robert S. Norris and Hans M. Kristensen. U.S. Nuclear Forces, 2006. Bulletin of the Atomic Scientists. January/February 2006.

[62] Ibid.

oceans, so that a greater number of emerging targets would be within range of the submarines in a short amount of time.

Warhead Loadings

The Trident II (D-5) missiles can be equipped to carry up to eight warheads each. Under the terms of the original START Treaty, the United States could remove warheads from Trident missiles, and reduce the number listed in the database, a process known as downloading, to comply with the treaty's limit of 6,000 warheads. The United States took advantage of this provision as it reduced its forces under START, reducing to six warheads per missile on the eight Trident submarines based at Bangor, WA.[63]

During the George W. Bush Administration, the Navy further reduced the number of warheads on the Trident submarines so that the United States could reduce its forces to the 2,200 deployed warheads permitted under the 2002 Moscow Treaty. The United States did not have to reach this limit until 2012, but it had done so by 2009.

The United States may to continue to reduce the total numbers of warheads carried on its Trident missiles under the New START Treaty. Unlike START, which attributed the same number of warheads to each missile of a given type, regardless of whether some of the missiles carried fewer warheads, the United States can deploy different numbers of warheads on different missiles, and count only the actual warheads deployed on the force. This will allow each missile to be tailored to meet the mission assigned to that missile. The United States does not, however, need to indicate how many warheads are deployed on each missile at all times; it must simply report the total number of operationally deployed warheads on all of its strategic nuclear delivery vehicles. The parties will, however, have opportunities to confirm that actual number on a specific missile, with random, short-notice inspections. Moreover, the United States will not have to alter the platforms in the missiles, so it could restore warheads to its Trident missiles if circumstances changed.

Modernization Plans and Programs

The Navy initially planned to keep Trident submarines in service for 30 years, but has now extended that time period to 42 years. This extension reflects the judgment that ballistic missiles submarines would have operated with less demanding missions than attack submarines, and could, therefore, be expected to have a much longer operating life than the expected 30-year life of attack submarines. Therefore, since 1998, the Navy has assumed that each Trident submarine would have an expected operating lifetime of at least 42 years, with two 20-year operating cycles separated by a 2-year refueling overhaul.[64] With this schedule, the submarines will begin to retire from the fleet in 2027. The Navy has also pursued a number of programs to ensure that it has enough missiles to support this extended life for the submarines.

---

[63] Even though four of these submarines are being converted to SSGNs, they still count under the START Treaty because they still have SLBM launch tubes. Each of those tubes count as six warheads. See U.S. Department of State. Bureau of Verification, Compliance, and Implementation. START Aggregate Number of Strategic Offensive Arms. April 1, 2006.

[64] SSBN Ohio-Class FBM Submarines. GlobalSecurity.org.

Trident Missile Production and Life Extension

The Navy purchased 437 Trident II (D-5) missiles through FY2008, and planned to purchase an additional 24 missiles per year through FY2012, for a total force of 533 missiles. It is continuing to produce rocket motors, at a rate of around one per month, and to procure alternation kits (known as SPALTs) needed to meet the extended service life of the submarine. Although the Navy plans to deploy its submarines with only 240 ballistic missiles under New START, it needs the greater number of missiles to support the fleet throughout the their life-cycle. In addition, around 50 of the Trident missiles are available for use by Great Britain in its Trident submarines. The remainder would support the missile's test program throughout the life of the Trident system.

The Navy is also pursuing a life extension program for the Trident II missiles, so that they will remain capable and reliable throughout the 42-year life of the Trident submarines. As a result, the funding for the Trident II missile supported the purchase of additional solid rocket motors other critical components required to support the missile throughout its service life.

The Navy allocated $5.5 billion to the Trident II missile program in FY2008 and FY2009. This funding supported the purchase of an additional 36 Trident II missiles. The Navy spent $1.05 billion on Trident II modifications in FY2010 and requested $1.1 billion in FY2011. In FY2010, $294 million was allocated to the purchase of 24 new missiles, $154.4 million was allocated to missile support costs, and $597.7 million was allocated to the Trident II Life Extension program. In FY2011, the Navy requested $294.9 million for the purchase of 24 new missiles, $156.9 million to missile support costs, and $655.4 million to the Trident II Life Extension Program. The FY2012 budget included $1.3 billion for Trident II missile program. Within this total, $191 million was allocated to the purchase of 24 additional new missiles, $137.8 million was allocated to missile support costs, and $980 million was allocated to the Trident II Life Extension Program. This was the last year during which the Navy sought to purchase new Trident II missiles. The FY2013 budget requested $1.2 billion for the Trident II missile program. This total included $524 million for program production and support costs, and $700.5 million for the Trident II life extension program. The Navy requested $1.14 billion for this program area in FY2014. According to the Navy's budget documents, this allowed it to continue to purchase components, such as the alteration kits for the guidance and missile electronics systems and solid rocket motors for these missiles. It has requested $1.19 billion for FY2015.

W76 Warhead Life Extension

The overwhelming majority of Trident missiles are deployed with the MK4/W76 warhead, which, according to unclassified estimates, has a yield of 100 kilotons.[65] It is currently undergoing a life extension program (LEP) that is designed to enhance its capabilities. According to some reports, the Navy had initially planned to apply this program to around 25% of the W76 warheads, but has increased that plan to cover more than 60% of the stockpile. According to recent estimates, the Navy has deployed around 500 of a planned total of about 1,200 life-extended W76 warheads.[66] The LEP is intended to add 30 years to the warhead life "by refurbishing the nuclear explosive package, the arming, firing, and fusing system, the gas transfer system, and associated cables, elastomers, valves, pads, cushions, foam supports, telemetries, and other miscellaneous parts."

---

[65] Robert S. Norris and Hans M. Kristensen. U.S. Nuclear Forces, 2006. Bulletin of the Atomic Scientists. January/February 2006.

[66] Hans M. Kristensen and Robert S. Norris, "U.S. Nuclear Forces, 2013," March/April 2013, p. 81.

The FY2012 budget request for the Department of Energy included $259.2 million for the W76 LEP.

Several questions came up during the life extension program. For example, some weapons experts questioned whether the warhead's design is reliable enough to ensure that the warheads will explode at its intended yield.[67] In addition, in June 2006, an inspector general's report from the Department of Energy questioned the management practices at the National Nuclear Security Administration (NNSA), which is responsible for the LEP, arguing that management problems had led to delays and created cost overruns in the program. This raised questions about whether NNSA would be able to meet the September 2007 delivery date for the warhead,[68] and, when combined with other technical issues, delayed the delivery of the first W76 warhead until August 2008. The Navy accepted the first refurbished warhead into the stockpile in August 2009.[69] This program is scheduled to continue through FY2019.

The SSBN(X) Program

The Navy is currently conducting development and design work on a new class of ballistic missile submarines, known as the SSBN(X) program, that will replace the Ohio-class Trident submarines as they reach the end of their service lives.[70] The Trident submarines will begin to retire in 2027, and the Navy initially indicated that it would need the new submarines to begin to enter the fleet by 2029, before the number of Trident submarines falls below 12.[71] To do this, the Navy would have had to begin construction of its new submarine by 2019 so that it could begin to enter the fleet in 2029.[72] However, in the FY2013 budget request, the Navy indicated that it would delay the procurement of the new class of submarines by two years. As a result, the first new submarine will enter the fleet in 2031 and the number of SSBNs in the fleet will decline to 10 for most of the 2030s.

The SSBN(X) program received $497.4 million in research and development funding in the Navy's FY2010 budget. The Navy requested an additional $672.3 million in research and development funding for the program in its FY2011 budget proposal. The FY2012 budget included $1.07 billion to develop the SSBN(X). It expected to request $927.8 million in FY2013, with the funding of $29.4 billion between 2011 and 2020. However, with the delay of two years in the procurement of the first SSBN(X), the Navy budgeted only $565 million for the program in FY2013. It then budgeted $1.1 billion for FY2014 and requested 1.2 billion in FY2015.

The Navy had planned to begin the detailed design for the submarine and to begin advanced procurement of critical components in FY2015, with the seven-year construction period for the first submarine beginning in FY2019. This timeline has now been changed, in part to reduce near-

---

[67] Fleck, John. Flaws Seen in Sub-Launched Nuclear Warhead. Albuquerque Journal. July 8, 2004.

[68] Costa, Keith J. IG: Project Weaknesses put W-76 Warhead Refurbishment Plan at Risk. *InsideDefense.Com*, June 8, 2006.

[69] "Navy Receives First Refurbished W-76 Warheads," *Global Security Newswire*, November 6, 2009.

[70] For details on this program, see CRS Report R41129, *Navy Ohio Replacement (SSBN[X]) Ballistic Missile Submarine Program: Background and Issues for Congress*, by Ronald O'Rourke.

[71] Christopher J. Castelli, "Navy Confronts $80 Billion Cost of New Ballistic Missile Submarines," *Inside Defense*, November 3, 2009.

[72] RADM Stephen Johnson, Director, Navy Strategic Programs Office. Speech at the NDU/NDIA Seminar Series, June 23, 2009.

term costs, but also to reduce risks in the program. According to the Navy's FY2013 budget documents, it has delayed the development of the SSBN(X), and will now begin building the first hull in 2021, rather than 2019. At the same time, it will continue to support the joint U.S./United Kingdom development of a common missile compartment, which both nations will use in their new SSBNs.

The Navy initially estimated that each submarine in this program could cost $6 billion to $7 billion in FY2010 dollars. It has worked to redesign the submarine and reduce the costs, with the plan to hold each submarine to around $4.9 billion. Officials in the Navy and analysts outside government have expressed concerns about the cost of this program, and about the effect that these costs may have on the rest of the Navy's shipbuilding plans. A study by the Congressional Budget Office indicates that the SSBN(X) program could cost a total of $97-$102 billion, with $10-$15 billion for research and development and $87 billion for the procurement of 12 submarines.[73]

According to Navy officials, if the Navy funds this program through its current, planned shipbuilding budget, it would have to forgo the acquisition of up to 32 other naval vessels. In its most recent 30-year shipbuilding plan, released in early July 2014, the Navy noted the annual shipbuilding budget could reach $19.7 billion per year between 2025 and 2034, the years when the Navy would buy the new SSBNs. This is significantly higher than the historical average of $13 billion per year for shipbuilding. In its report, the Navy indicated that this program would cause "significant and noteworthy risks to the Navy's overall shipbuilding plan" and that the Navy would be unlikely to sustain this level of spending over the necessary time frame.[74] The annual shipbuilding budget would reach $24 billion per year by 2032, which represents a significant increase over the current level of around $13 billion per year. In response to this growing fiscal pressure, Admiral Richard Breckenridge suggested, in testimony offered in 2013, that Congress set up an annual $4 billion supplemental fund outside the Navy's budget to help support this program.[75] Several Members of Congress have supported this proposal[76] and hope to include language in support of it in the FY2015 National Defense Authorization Act.

As a part of its effort to reduce costs, the Navy is designing the new submarines with only 16 ballistic missile launch tubes. The existing Trident submarines have 24 launch tubes, and each currently carries 24 missiles, although the Navy plans to reduce this number to 20 missiles on each submarine as the United States reduces its forces to comply with the New START Treaty. Congress questioned the Navy on this plan during hearings in April 2011, with some Members questioning whether the United States would be able to deploy enough warheads if it reduced the numbers of missiles on each submarine. Admiral Terry Benedict, the Director of the Navy's Strategic Systems Program Office, testified that the current international security environment, along with the Navy's ability to "upload" warheads onto Trident missiles, convinced him, along with other Navy and STRATCOM officials, that they could be comfortable with this

---

[73] Congressional Budget Office, *An Analysis of the Navy's Fiscal Year 2014 Shipbuilding Plan*, Washington, DC, October 2013, p. 24, http://www.cbo.gov/publication/44655.

[74] Jason Sherman, "New Sub Charts Course to "Unsustainable" Shipbuilding Spending, Peaks at $24 billion," *Inside Defense*, July 5, 2014.

[75] Lee Hudson, "Navy Asks Congress To Set Up Supplemental Fund for SSBN(X)," *InsideDefense.com*, September 12, 2013.

[76] "Some U.S. Lawmakers Eye Funding new Submarines Outside Normal Process," *Global Security Newswire*, March 12, 2014. See, also, Lee Hudson, "House Committee Looks to Create Separate Fund for Ohio Replacement," *InsideDefense.com*, May 2, 2014.

configuration.[77] However, Congress remained unconvinced. In the FY2012 Defense Authorization Act, it called for a new study of the plans for the SSBN(X). Congress indicated that the report should consider the possibility of deploying 10 or 12 submarines with 16 launch tubes on each and 8 or 10 submarines with 20 launch tubes on each. Moreover, the study was to review not only the cost of each option, but also the ability of each option to meet the Navy's at-sea requirements for the SSBN force and the ability of each option to meet the nation's nuclear employment and planning guidance.[78]

A report published in late 2011 indicated that the Office of Management and Budget (OMB) suggested that the Navy reduce the number of SSBNs in the fleet to 10, but increase the number of launch tubes on each submarine to 20.[79] According to the OMB analysis, this could save the Navy $7 billion over the life of the fleet, by reducing acquisition costs and operating costs. It would not, however, undermine the submarines' mission because, with 20 missiles per submarine, the Navy would still be able to cover the full range of targets assigned to the Trident fleet. Analysts outside government have offered similar suggestions, noting that the Navy could save $27 billion over 10 years and $120 billion over the life of the fleet if the Navy built 8, rather than 12 submarines.[80] Moreover, according to this analysis, the Navy would be able to deploy the necessary number of warheads on these submarines, even if it did not increase the number of launch tubes, by deploying more warheads on each of the Trident missiles on the submarine.

Generally, the number of launch tubes on the submarines should not affect the number of warheads carried by each submarine or the ability of the fleet to hold a range of potential targets at risk. Trident missiles can be equipped with 8 warheads each, but, in their current configuration, with 24 missiles on each submarine, the missiles carry only 4 or 5 warheads each, on average. This number would drop to 3-4 warheads per missile, on average, as the United States reduced to the levels in New START. If the new submarines carry only 16 missiles, rather than the 20 planned under New START, then they could deploy with 5-6 warheads per missile. In essence, the Navy would put the same number of warheads on each submarine, but would just spread them over a smaller number of missiles.

The Navy has noted that, as the United States reduces its forces to New START levels, the lower number of missiles per submarine will allow the United States to retain a larger number of submarines, without exceeding the treaty's limit of 700 operational delivery vehicles. This will allow the Navy to maintain a fleet of 12 submarines, and to operate those submarines with continuous deployments from 2 bases. The Navy has argued that, if it alters reduces the numbers of submarines in the fleet, and alters its deployment patterns, it will not be able to meet its requirements, as these cover more than just the total number of warheads on the fleet or total number of warheads at sea at any time. Critics outside the government, however, question this approach, both because a fleet of 12 submarines will cost more to procure and operate than a fleet of only 8 submarines and because this fleet presumes that the United States must retain its current pattern of operations for the SSBN fleet for the next 50-60 years.

---

[77] Emelie Rutherford, "Navy Defends Plan for Just 16 Missile Tubes on Next Boomer," *Defense Daily*, April 7, 2011.

[78] Elaine M. Grossman, "U.S. Defense Conference Bill Seeks New Submarine Cost Assessment," *Global Security Newswire*, December 16, 2011.

[79] Colin Clark, "OMB Pushes More Tubes, Fewer Boats for Ohio Replacement Subs," *AOL Defense*, November 4, 2011, http://defense.aol.com/2011/11/04/omb-pushes-more-tubes-fewer-boats-for-ohio-replacement-subs/.

[80] Tom Collina and Kelsey Davenport, "U.S. Must Rethink New Subs, Bombers," *Defense News*, October 24, 2011.

With 12 submarines in the fleet, the Navy can maintain 4-5 on station at any time, patrolling in areas where they would need to be to launch their missiles promptly after a presidential order. But critics question whether this pattern, and the "continuous at-sea" deterrent of 4-5 submarines, will be necessary in the decades ahead. They note that the United States will be able to maintain a secure second strike deterrent on the submarines, even if they cannot launch as many warheads promptly as they can launch today. Others however, continue to support the current operational patterns, and to argue for a fleet of 12 submarines into the future. For example, Congress, in the FY2013 Defense Authorization Bill (P.L. 112-239, §130) stated that "the continuous at-sea deterrence provided by a robust and modern fleet of nuclear-powered ballistic missile submarines is critical to maintaining nuclear deterrence and assurance and therefore is a central pillar of the national security of the United States." The legislation went on to indicate that "a minimum of 12 replacement ballistic missile submarines are necessary to provide continuous at-sea deterrence over the lifetime of such submarines...."

Bombers

B-1 Bomber

The Air Force began to deploy the B-1 bomber in the mid-1980s and eventually deployed a fleet of 96 aircraft. After several crashes, the Air Force was left with 92 bombers in 2001. It has sought to retire 30 of the aircraft, leaving a force of 62 bombers, but has met resistance from Congress. The B-1 served exclusively as a nuclear delivery vehicle through 1991, carrying short-range attack missiles and gravity bombs. Because these bombers were not equipped to carry nuclear-armed air-launched cruise missiles, each counts as a single delivery vehicle and a single warhead under START. In 1993, the Air Force began to convert the B-1 bombers to carry conventional weapons. This process was completed in 1997 and the B-1 bomber is no longer equipped to carry nuclear weapons, although it still counts against the START limits. Neither the bomber nor its weapons count against the limits in the Moscow Treaty. The bomber has contributed to U.S. conventional operations in Afghanistan and Iraq.

B-2 Bomber

The Air Force has 20 B-2 bombers, which are based at Whiteman AFB in Missouri.[81] The B-2 bomber can carry both B-61 and B-83 nuclear bombs, but is not equipped to carry cruise missiles. It can also carry conventional weapons and has participated in U.S. military campaigns from Bosnia to Iraq. It is designed as a "low observable" aircraft and was intended to improve the U.S. ability to penetrate Soviet air defenses. However, according to recent reports, the Air Force has contemplated modifying the bomber so that it can also serve as a standoff-capable platform. In October 2009, General Donald Alston, the Assistant Chief of the Air Force for Strategic Deterrence and Nuclear Integration, indicated that the B-2 would need significant upgrades to contribute to this mission.[82]

---

[81] A B-2 bomber crashed on take-off from Anderson Air Force Base on Guam in late February 2008, reducing the number of deployed bombers from 21 to 20.

[82] Marina Malenic, "With Nex-Gen Bomber in Holding Pattern, Air Force Wants Further B-2 Mods," *Defense Daily*, October 21, 2009.

Weapons

According to unclassified estimates, the United States has around 550 B-61 and B-83 bombs.[83] The B61-11, a modification developed in the 1990s, has a hardened, modified case so that it can penetrate some hardened targets, although probably not those encased in steel and concrete. The B-83 bomb is a high yield weapon that is also designed to destroy hardened targets, such as ICBM silos. The B61-Mod 7, along with the Mod-3 and Mod-4 versions, are a part of an ongoing life extension program that will produce a new B61-mod 12 bomb.[84]

Congress has raised numerous questions about the need for and the costs of the B61 life extension program. For example, in the FY2010 Energy and Water Appropriations Bills, Congress reduced funding for this program and limited the available funding to modifications of the bombs' non-nuclear components. These restrictions were reportedly designed to slow the program until the Administration reported, through the Nuclear Posture review, on its future plans for U.S. nuclear weapons programs.[85]

The Obama Administration strongly supported the life extension program for the B-61 bomb in the Nuclear Posture Review. The report indicated that "the Administration will fully fund the full scope LEP study and follow-on activities for the B-61 bomb ... to ensure first production begins in FY2017." The NPR noted that the life extension program for the B-61 bomb, which would include enhancing safety, security, and use control, would also support U.S. extended deterrence goals by allowing the United States to retain the capability to forward-deploy U.S. nuclear weapons on B-2 bombers and tactical fighter-bombers.[86] In the years since the NPR, however, the costs for the program have risen sharply and the timeline has slipped. Where DOE initially claimed that the program would cost around $4 billion, it now estimates the cost to be over $8 billion.[87] In addition, it now expects the first unit to be available in 2020, rather than 2017. Some in Congress have challenged the Administration's plans for this program, asking whether a less costly and complicated program might be sufficient. The Administration has claimed, however, that if it pursued a less complex life extension program now, it would need to initiate a second program a few years later to complete the remainder of the work. Moreover, the Administration has noted that, after it completes this program, DOE will be able to retire the much larger B83 bomb and reduce the number of B61 bombs in the U.S. stockpile.

The Air Force is also designing a new tail kit for the B61 bomb. This tail kit would replace the parachute that the bomb currently uses to slow to its targets, and would improve the accuracy of the weapon. Some analysts claim that this tail kit would provide the bomb with new capabilities, and would undermine the Obama Administration's pledge that it would not develop new military capabilities as it conducted the warhead life extension programs. Others, however, dispute this conclusion. The Air Force has argued that the tail kit will the modified B61 bombs to meet

---

[83] Robert S. Norris and Hans M. Kristensen. U.S. Nuclear Forces, 2006. Bulletin of the Atomic Scientists. January/February 2006.

[84] For a description of ongoing work in the B61 LEP program, see Kevin Robinson-Avila, "Overhauling the nation's nuclear arsenal: Sandia National Labs achieves B61 milestone," *Albuquerque Journal*, May 18, 2014.

[85] Elaine M. Grossman, "Nuclear Bomb Update Effort Slowed by Posture Review, Science Studies," *Global Security Newswire*, January 19, 2010.

[86] U.S. Department of Defense, *Nuclear Posture Review*, Washington, DC, April 6, 2010, p. 27, http://www.defense.gov/npr/docs/2010%20Nuclear%20Posture%20Review%20Report.pdf.

[87] Jeff Tolleson, "U.S. warheads to get a facelift," *Nature*, May 7, 2013.

operational requirements for the bomber fleet and provide "nuclear assurance to U.S. allies in Europe."

The Administration requested and Congress appropriated $537 million for the B-61 LEP in FY2014; it has requested an additional $643 million in FY2015. The Air Force has also requested $198.4 million for the tail kit program in FY2015, an increase of more than $165 million over the FY2014 appropriation of $33 million.

B-52 Bomber

The Air Force maintains 78 B-52H aircraft at two bases, Barksdale, LA, and Minot, ND.[88] The B-52 bomber, which first entered service in 1961, is equipped to carry nuclear or conventional air-launched cruise missiles and nuclear-armed advanced cruise missiles. The B-52 bombers can also deliver a wide range of conventional arms, and are currently receiving numerous upgrades to their communications and electronics systems.

The Air Force has proposed cutting the B-52 fleet on many occasions in the last 15 years. For example, when the United States identified the force structure that it would deploy under the START Treaty, it indicated that it would only seek to retain 76 B-52 bombers. Congress, however, rejected the Clinton Administration's proposal, and the United States retained the full fleet of 94 aircraft.

The 2006 Quadrennial Defense Review called for a significant change to the B-52 fleet, reducing it from 94 to 56 aircraft. The budget request for FY2007 indicated that the Air Force planned to retire 18 bombers in FY2007 and 20 in FY2008. At the same time, the QDR called for continuing improvements to the B-1, B-2, and B-52 bombers' conventional capabilities using the funds that were saved by the retirement of the 38 aircraft. The Air Force has argued that it can reduce the number of deployed bombers, without reducing the overall capabilities of the bomber fleet, because these new weapons have "raised the efficiency" of the bomber platform. At hearings before the Senate Armed Services Committee, General James E. Cartwright, the Commander of STRATCOM, noted that "the next generation weapons that we're fielding, these air-launched cruise missiles, the joint direct attack munitions, et cetera, are much more efficient than they were in the past."[89] General Cartwright also indicated that, in spite of the reduced size of the fleet, the Air Force would continue to deploy B-52 bombers at two bases.

During the FY2007 budget cycle, Congress rejected the Pentagon's proposals for at least part of the B-52 fleet. The House, in its version of the FY2007 Defense Authorization Bill, prohibited the Air Force from retiring any of the B-52 aircraft, and mandated that it maintain at least 44 "combat coded" aircraft until the Air Force began to replace the B-52 with a new bomber of equal or greater capability. It stated, as a part of its rationale for this rejection, that it appeared the reduction was based on the reduced need for nuclear-capable bombers and did not take into consideration a growing need for long-range conventional strike capabilities.[90] The Senate agreed to permit the Air Force to retire 18 B-52 aircraft, but stated that it expected no further reduction in

---

[88] A B-52 bomber crashed off the coast of Guam in July 2008.

[89] U.S. Senate, Committee on Armed Services, Hearing on Global Strike Plans and Programs. Testimony of James E. Cartwright, Commander U.S. Strategic Command. March 29, 2006.

[90] U.S. Congress. House. Committee on Armed Services. National Defense Authorization Act for Fiscal Year 2007. H.Rept. 109-452. May 5, 2006. p. 103.

the size of the force, noting that a further reductions might "prevent our ability to strike the required conventional target set during times of war."[91] The conference committee (H.R. 5122, §131) combined these two provisions, allowing the retirement of no more than 18 aircraft after the submission of a report, and mandating that the Air Force retain at least 44 "combat coded" aircraft. These restrictions are to remain in place until 2018, or until a new long-range strike aircraft "with equal or greater capability than the B-52H model aircraft" attained initial operational capability, if that occurred first. Congress also stated that no funds could be spent to retire any B-52 aircraft until the Secretary of the Air Force submitted a report to Congress that described the Air Force plan for the modernization of the B-52, B-1, and B-2 bomber fleets; how many bombers would be assigned two nuclear and conventional missions if the United States had to execute "two overlapping 'swift defeat' campaigns"; a justification of the cost and projected savings of any reductions to the B-52H bomber aircraft fleet; and the life expectancy of each bomber aircraft to remain in the bomber force structure and the capabilities of the bomber force structure that would be replaced by a new bomber aircraft.

The Air Force indicated that the report on the bomber fleet would be ready in the fall of 2007. Further, in testimony before the Armed Services Committee, the Air Force indicated that it still planned to reduce the B-52 fleet to 56 aircraft, with 32 combat coded aircraft included in the fleet. But, in recognition of the congressional mandate, it was seeking a way to maintain 44 combat coded aircraft, the minimum set by Congress, within the smaller fleet of 56 aircraft. It also stated that it planned to store the 20 aircraft it wanted to retire in FY2008 on ramps at Barksdale Air Force Base; the aircraft would be kept in serviceable condition, but would not receive any capabilities upgrades.[92] Congress once again rejected this proposal. In the FY2008 Defense Authorization Bill (H.R. 1585, §137), Congress mandated that the Air Force maintain a fleet of 74 B-52 bombers, with no less than 63 in the Primary Aircraft inventory and 11 backup aircraft. Two additional aircraft would be designated as "attrition reserve." The conference committee indicated that the members agreed that a fleet of fewer than 76 aircraft would be insufficient to meet long-range strike requirements.

The growing interest in long-range strike capabilities, and the continuing addition of precision conventional weapons to these aircraft, demonstrates that the Pentagon and STRATCOM view the U.S. bomber fleet as essential to U.S. conventional weapons capabilities. Further, the need for long-range strike capabilities, rather than an interest in maintaining the nuclear role for bombers,[93] appeared to be driving decisions about the size and structure of the bomber fleet. There are some indications that, during the discussions on the 2006 QDR, some in the Pentagon argued that the all the B-52 bombers should be removed from the nuclear mission. Moreover, in November 2008, Secretary of the Air Force Michael Donley noted that the role that the bombers play in nuclear deterrence could be reduced in the future, if the United States and Russia negotiate further reductions in their nuclear arsenals.

This focus began to shift, however, in 2008. Several recent studies have noted that a lack of attention paid in the Air Force and, more broadly, in DOD, to the bombers' nuclear mission seems

---

[91] U.S. Congress Senate. National Defense Authorization Act for Fiscal Year 2007. S.Rept. 109-254. May 9, 2006. p. 94.

[92] U.S. Congress. Senate. Armed Services Committee, Subcommittee on Strategic Forces. Hearing on the Fiscal Year 2008 Strategic Forces Program Budget. Statement of Major General Roger Burg. March 28, 2007. p. 8.

[93] Carlo Munoz, "Donley: Role of Nuclear Bomber Fleet Could Be Curtailed," *Inside the Air Force*, November 14, 2008.

to be one of the factors that led to the episode in August 2007, when a B-52 bomber flew from Minot to Barksdale with six cruise missiles that carried live nuclear warheads.[94] The Air Force is pursuing a number of organizational and procedural changes to increase its focus on the nuclear mission and "reinvigorate" its nuclear enterprise. For example, it has "stood-up" a B-52 bomber squadron that will focus specifically on the nuclear mission.[95] This new unit would add 10 bombers to the 12 already deployed at Minot. While all the B-52 bomber crews and aircraft will retain their nuclear roles, this added squadron will participate in a greater number of nuclear exercises and training missions. The aircraft in the squadron will rotate from other missions, but will remain designated as the nuclear squadron for full year. The Air Force hopes this construct will improve not only the operational proficiency of the crews, but also their morale and their confidence in the value of the nuclear mission.

With this change, Secretary of Defense Gates stated, in April 2009, that the Air Force planned to retain 76 B-52 bombers. The 2010 Nuclear Posture Review also indicated that the United States currently has 76 B-52 bombers equipped to carry nuclear weapons. It determined that the Air Force would retain nuclear-capable bombers, but it would also convert some B-52s to a conventional-only role. The 1251 report also indicates that the Air Force plans to retain the B-52 bombers in the fleet through at least 2035, to meet both nuclear and conventional mission requirements.

In the report on the New START force structure issued in April 2014, the Obama Administration indicated that the United States would retain 42 deployed and 4 nondeployed nuclear capable B-52 bombers. The remainder of the B-52 bombers would be converted to carry only conventional weapons.

Weapons

The B-52 bomber was equipped to carry both the Air-Launched cruise missile (ALCM) and Advanced Cruise Missile (ACM). The ACM reportedly had a modified design with a lower radar cross-section, making it more "stealthy" than the ALCM. According to Air Force figures, in 2006, the United States had 1,142 ALCMs and 394 ACMs.[96] Although these weapons represented a majority of the weapons that U.S. bombers could carry on nuclear missions, the Department of Defense decided to retire many of these missiles. In his statement to the Senate Armed Services Committee's Subcommittee on Strategic Forces, Major General Roger Burg indicated that this study had concluded, and the Secretary of Defense had directed, that the Air Force retire all the Advanced Cruise Missiles, although some could be converted to carry conventional warheads, and reduce the ALCM fleet to 528 cruise missiles. The excess ALCMs will also be eliminated, with the remaining missiles consolidated at Minot Air Force Base. With all the ALCMs consolidated at Minot Air Force Base, the bombers at Barksdale may no longer be included in the nuclear mission.

---

[94] For a detailed review of this incident see, Warrick, Joby and Walter Pincus. The Saga of a Bent Spear. *Washington Post*. September 23, 2007.

[95] Marcus Weisgerber, "USAF To Activate Rotational Nuclear Bomber Squadron Next Month," *Inside Defense*, September 26, 2008.

[96] The Air Force also has 289 ALCMs that have been converted to carry conventional warheads (CALCMs). See Michael Sirak. DOD Studies Future Role of Nuclear-Armed Cruise Missiles. Defense Daily, March 30, 2006.

The Air Force plans to sustain the ALCM in the fleet through 2030. It is then planning to replace the ALCM with a new advanced long range standoff (LRSO) cruise missile. It completed an analysis of alternatives (AOA) for this system in May 2013. According to DOD, the AOA will "define the platform requirements, provide cost-sensitive comparisons, validate threats, and establish measures of effectiveness, and assess candidate systems for eventual procurement and production" of the new missile.[97] The DOD budget request for FY2014 contained $5 million for the Air Force to begin systems engineering support for the program. The budget also indicated that the technology development phase would begin in FY2014, and that the funding requests could reach a total of $1 billion through FY2014.

In the FY2015 budget request, DOD indicates that the plans for the LRSO missile have slipped by three years. This change is a result of fiscal constraints and the need to fund higher priorities elsewhere in the nuclear force. As a result, although the Air Force has requested an additional $4.9 million for this program in FY2015, it now plans to spend $221 million over the next five years, in contrast with the $1.04 billion it planned to spend before the delay. The Air Force still hopes to begin initial production of the new cruise missile by the late 2020s, so that it can replace the ALCM as it is retired from the force.

Future Bomber Plans

As the preceding discussion noted, the United States currently deploys two types of heavy bombers—the B-2 and B-52—that can deliver both nuclear and conventional weapons. A third bomber, the B-1, was initially equipped to deliver nuclear weapons but is now exclusively dedicated to conventional missions. The Air Force has employed all three aircraft in conventional conflicts over the past two decades, and all have received upgrades to sustain their capabilities, but all three are aging and, according to many in the Air Force, may not be sufficient to meet emerging challenges.

As a result, the Air Force has also begun develop a new strategic bomber. When it began this effort nearly a decade ago, it hoped to introduce the new bomber into the fleet around 2018. At the time, it was seeking a bomber with not only stealth capabilities and long range, but also one with "persistence," one that could "stay airborne and on call for very long periods."[98] However, the start of the study on a new bomber, known as an Analysis of Alternatives (AOA), was delayed by a dispute over whether the study should stand alone or be merged with another AOA on prompt global strike (PGS) capabilities, such as hypersonic technologies and missiles.[99] General James Cartwright, the former head of STRATCOM, reportedly supported a plan to merge the two efforts, so that the considerations of capabilities for a new bomber would be measured alongside other systems, both to balance the force and avoid redundancy across the force.[100] On the other hand, the former Air Force Chief of Staff, General T. Michael Moseley, reportedly preferred to keep the two studies separate. He argued that a bomber with long-range strike capabilities must

---

[97] U.S. Department of Defense, *November 2010 Update to the National Defense Authorization Act of FY2010*, New START Treaty Framework and Nuclear Force Structure Plans, Washington, DC, November 17, 2010, p. 12. http://www.lasg.org/CMRR/Sect1251_update_17Nov2010.pdf.

[98] Christie, Rebecca. Air Force To Step Up New Bomber Search in Next Budget. *Wall Street Journal*. June 29, 2006.

[99] For details on these types of systems, see CRS Report R41464, *Conventional Prompt Global Strike and Long-Range Ballistic Missiles: Background and Issues*, by Amy F. Woolf.

[100] Grossman, Elaine M. Cartwright Wants to See Strike Studies Await "Discovery" Process. InsideDefense.Com. April 6, 2006.0

have "persistent, survivable, and penetrating capabilities" while a platform with PGS capabilities could be "standoff weapon that is very, very fast."[101] This position reportedly prevailed, with the Air Force deciding, in May 2006, to keep the two studies separate.[102]

This dispute revealed wide-ranging differences, within the Air Force and Pentagon, about the goals for and capabilities that should be sought in a new bomber program.[103] The dispute focused, however, on conventional capabilities; it seemed to be almost a foregone conclusion that nuclear capabilities, or the need for a bomber leg of the nuclear triad, would not drive the discussion or analysis. This position remains true today, with the Air Force seeking a new bomber to meet conventional challenges, and considering delaying the introduction of nuclear capabilities to save money. But disagreements over the capabilities needed, even for the conventional mission, served to delay the new bomber program by several years.

In May 2007, the Air Force indicated that it had decided that the next generation bomber would be manned and subsonic, although it would incorporate some stealth characteristics.[104] It decided that it would not pursue supersonic capabilities, or an unmanned option, to contain costs and maintain the capabilities of the future aircraft. However, on April 6, 2009, in a briefing describing the FY2010 defense budget, Secretary of Defense Robert Gates delayed the program and indicated that the Air Force would not proceed until it had "a better understanding of the need, the requirement and the technology."[105] He suspended the program until DOD completed the QDR and Nuclear Posture Review.

The 2010 Quadrennial Defense Review, published in February 2010, indicated that the Air Force was "reviewing options for fielding survivable, long-range surveillance and strike aircraft as part of a comprehensive, phased plan to modernize the bomber force."[106] The report also noted that Secretary of Defense Gates ordered a follow-on study to the QDR to determine "what combination of joint persistent surveillance, electronic warfare, and precision-attack capabilities, including both penetrating platforms and stand-off weapons, will best support U.S. power projection operations over the next two to three decades." Although the study was just beginning, the DOD budget request for 2011 included $200 million for the new bomber, and DOD documents indicated that expenditures on the bomber could total $1.74 billion through 2015.[107] Secretary Gates indicated that he expected the Air Force to field the next generation bomber in the late 2020s.[108]

---

[101] Bennet, John T. Internal Squabbles Holding Up Bomber Study, USAF Official Says. InsideDefense.com. April 21, 2006.

[102] Matishak, Martin. Long-Range, Prompt Global Strike Studies Will Remain Separate. InsideDefense.com. June 16, 2006.

[103] For more details on the proposed bomber, see CRS Report RL34406, *Air Force Next-Generation Bomber: Background and Issues for Congress*, by Jeremiah Gertler.

[104] Sirak, Michael. Air Force Identifies Manned, Subsonic Bomber as Most Promising 2018 Option. Defense Today. May 2, 2007.

[105] U.S. Department of Defense, *Briefing by Defense Secretary Robert Gates and Marine Corps Gen. James Cartwright, Vice Chairman of the Joint Chiefs of Staff*, Washington, DC, April 6, 2009, http://insidedefense.com/ secure/data_extra/html3/dplus2009_0893_3 htm.

[106] U.S. Department of Defense, *Quadrennial Defense Review Report*, Washington, DC, February 2010, p. 33, http://www.defense.gov/qdr/images/QDR_as_of_12Feb10_1000.pdf.

[107] Elaine M. Grossman, "Pentagon Eyes More than $800 Million for New Nuclear Cruise Missile," *Global Security Newswire*, March 9, 2010.

[108] Andrea Shalal-Esa, "Gates Sees New U.S. Bomber Fielded in 2020s," *Reuters*, February 2, 2010.

The update to the 1251 Report, submitted to the Senate before its vote on the New START Treaty in late 2010, emphasized that the United States would maintain the bomber leg of the strategic triad and that DOD was committed to modernizing the bomber force. The report noted that the long-range strike study was not questioning whether the United States would pursue a new heavy bomber, but "the appropriate type of bomber and the timelines for development, production, and deployment."[109] The report indicated that this study would advise the President's budget submission for FY2012. Air Force officials echoed this, noting that Secretary Gates seemed inclined to accept the Air Force's recommendations on the building of a new long-range bomber.[110] Secretary Gates confirmed this approach in January 2011, when he announced the Air Force would develop a new bomber "using proven technologies," and that this bomber would be nuclear-capable.[111] The Pentagon requested $197 million in the FY2012 budget on a new bomber. The budget documents indicate that the bomber will be nuclear-capable, and that the Air Force was planning to spend $3.7 billion on its development over the next five years.

Air Force officials indicate that they hope to field between 80 and 100 of the new bombers in the future, with the first to enter service around 2025. It has indicated that it plans to hold the procurement cost for each bomber to $550 million, with the total cost of the program to reach $36 billion-$56 billion. However, it has recently acknowledged that this cost does not include research and development funding,[112] which, according to some estimates, could amount to between $20 and $45 billion if the program follows the trends set by previous bomber programs.[113]

The Air Force expects funding requests for the new bomber to rise sharply over the next five years. Congress appropriated $259 million for R&D on this aircraft in FY2013 and $$359.4 in FY2014; the Air Force has requested $913.7 million in FY2015. It plans to spend a total of $11.4 billion between FY2015 and FY2019.[114] These requests are sufficient to keep the bomber program on track but lead to Air Force spending levels that exceed the levels set by the 2011 Budget Control Act. According to one recent analysis, the Air Force would likely need to reduce its other acquisition programs to find the "budget headroom" for this program.[115]

The Air Force has indicated that a new bomber is essential to its future plans for the conventional long-range strike mission. It has stated that it is "committed to modernizing bomber capacity and capabilities to support LRS (long range strike) military options." It indicated that the new bomber "must be able to penetrate the increasingly dense anti-access/area denial environments developing around the world." The Air Force has, in the past, stated that this bomber will be designed to deliver nuclear weapons. However, in October 2011, the Chief of Staff of the Air Force indicated

---

[109] U.S. Department of Defense, *November 2010 Update to the National Defense Authorization Act of FY2010*, New START Treaty Framework and Nuclear Force Structure Plans, Washington, DC, November 17, 2010, p. 11. http://www.lasg.org/CMRR/Sect1251_update_17Nov2010.pdf.

[110] Emelie Rutherford, "Schwartz Hopeful About Long-Range Strike Funding," *Defense Daily*, November 29, 2010.

[111] Marcus Weisgerber, "Air Force To Develop New Long-Range, Optionally Manned Bomber," *Inside the Air Force*, January 6, 2011.

[112] Aaron Mehta, "USAF General: "Of Course" Bomber Will Be More Than $550M per Copy," *Defense News*, March 5, 2014.

[113] Jon B. Wolfsthal, Jeffrey Lewis, and Marc Quint, *The Trillion Dollar Nuclear Triad*, James Martin Center for Nonproliferation Studies, Monterey, CA, January 2014, pp. 18-19. http://cns miis.edu/opapers/pdfs/140107_trillion_dollar_nuclear_triad.pdf.

[114] Tony Cappaccio, "Long-Range Bomber's Development would Get $12 Billion from U.S.," *Bloomberg News*, March 6, 2014.

[115] Colin Clark, "LRS-B, Next Boomer May Force Weapons Cuts," *Breaking Defense*, September 4, 2014.

that the new bomber probably would not include nuclear capabilities initially, but would add them in as the B-2 and B-52 bombers retired from the fleet.

Issues for Congress

This report focuses on the numbers and types of weapons in the U.S. strategic nuclear force structure. It does not address the broader question of why the United States chooses to deploy these numbers and types of weapons, or more generally, the role that U.S. nuclear weapons play in U.S. national security strategy. This question is addressed in other CRS reports.[116] However, as the Obama Administration reviews and possibly revises the plans for U.S. nuclear force structure, Congress could address broader questions about the relationship between these forces and the role of nuclear weapons.

Force Size

The Bush Administration argued that, because the United States and Russia were no longer enemies, the United States would not size or structure its nuclear forces simply to deter the "Russian threat." Instead, nuclear weapons would play a broader role in U.S. national security strategy. The Obama Administration, in contrast, noted that there is a relationship between the size of the U.S. arsenal and the size of the Russian arsenal. The 2010 NPR states that

> Russia's nuclear force will remain a significant factor in determining how much and how fast we are prepared to reduce U.S. forces. Because of our improved relations, the need for strict numerical parity between the two countries is no longer as compelling as it was during the Cold War. But large disparities in nuclear capabilities could raise concerns on both sides and among U.S. allies and partners, and may not be conducive to maintaining a stable, long-term strategic relationship, especially as nuclear forces are significantly reduced.[117]

The Bush Administration's 2001 Nuclear Posture Review determined that the United States would need to maintain between 1,700 and 2,200 operationally deployed nuclear warheads. The Bush Administration also indicated that the United States would maintain in storage many of the warheads removed from deployed forces, and would maintain the capability to restore some of these warheads to the deployed forces to meet unexpected contingencies. The Obama Administration concluded, in its NPR, that the United States could reduce its forces to 1,550 deployed warheads, and agreed to do so under the New START Treaty, but it also planned to retain the capability to restore warheads to its deployed forces. It also plans to retain many warheads in storage, although it has indicated that the size of the total stockpile could decline as the United States reduces its deployed forces to the New START limits.[118]

---

[116] See, for example, CRS Report RL31623, *U.S. Nuclear Weapons: Changes in Policy and Force Structure*, by Amy F. Woolf.

[117] U.S. Department of Defense, *Nuclear Posture Review*, Washington, DC, April 6, 2010, p. 30, http://www.defense.gov/npr/docs/2010%20Nuclear%20Posture%20Review%20Report.pdf.

[118] On May 3, 2010, the Obama Administration announced that the United States has 5,113 warheads in its stockpile of nuclear weapons. This number includes the deployed warheads, active nondeployed warheads and inactive nondeployed warheads. For more information, see http://www.defense.gov/npr/docs/10-05-03_Fact_Sheet_US_Nuclear_Transparency__FINAL_w_Date.pdf.

The Obama Administration has also indicated that the United States may be able to reduce its numbers of deployed and nondeployed warheads further, but that it should do so in parallel with Russia. It indicated, in the 2010 NPR, that "large disparities in nuclear capabilities could raise concerns on both sides and among U.S. allies and partners, and may not be conducive to maintaining a stable, long-term strategic relationship."[119] In June 2013, the Department of Defense completed a new study, as a follow-up to the NPR, to determine how deeply the United States might reduce its forces, and how it should deploy the remaining forces. Press reports indicate the Pentagon reviewed a number of alternatives in this study, with some contemplating reductions as low as 300 warheads,[120] but the Administration concluded that the United States could reduce U.S. deployed strategic forces by about one-third, to a level of 1,000-1,100 warheads, if it did so along with Russia. They United States would not proceed with unilateral cuts in the U.S. arsenal.[121]

Some analysts have questioned why the United States must maintain such a large force of nuclear weapons. They have questioned whether the United States would attack with such a large number of weapons if its own national survival were not at risk, and they note that only Russia currently has the capability to threaten U.S. national survival. They assert that the United States could likely meet any other potential contingency with a far smaller force of nuclear weapons. Some have concluded, instead, that the United States could maintain its security with a force of between 500 and 1,000 warheads.[122] Others, however, dispute this view and note that the United States has other potential adversaries, and, even if these nations do not possess thousands of nuclear warheads, some may expand their nuclear forces or chemical and biological capabilities in the future. Some have argued that the also needs to assure its allies of its commitment to their security, and this goal could require a force of significant size, regardless of the number of potential targets an adversary nation might possess.

Force Structure

When the Bush Administration announced the results of the 2001 Nuclear Posture Review, it indicated that the United States would retain a triad of ICBMs, SLBMs, and heavy bombers for the foreseeable future. The Obama Administration also offered continuing support for the retention of the strategic triad. Nevertheless, as the Obama Administration has outlined plans to modernize and replace the delivery vehicles in all three legs of the strategic triad, many analysts have begun to question whether the United States can afford to retain the triad and whether it can retain a robust deterrent without one of the current types of strategic delivery vehicles.[123]

The Obama Administration indicated, in the 2010 NPR, that the United States would convert some of its bombers to conventional-only missions. This is consistent with the view, among some analysts, that, in the future, the bombers may be more important in the conventional mission. As was noted above, most discussions about the bomber force focus on how many bombers, and

---

[119] U.S. Department of Defense, *Nuclear Posture Review*, Washington, DC, April 6, 2010, p. 30, http://www.defense.gov/npr/docs/2010%20Nuclear%20Posture%20Review%20Report.pdf.

[120] R. Jeffrey Smith, "Obama Embraces Big Nuke Cuts," *Foreign Policy*, February 8, 2013.

[121] U.S. Department of Defense, *Report on Nuclear Employment Strategy of the United States*, Washington, DC, June 12, 2013, p. 6, http://www.defense.gov/pubs/reporttoCongressonUSNuclearEmploymentStrategy_Section491.pdf.

[122] See, for example, Sidney D. Drell and James E. Goodby. What Are Nuclear Weapons For? Recommendations for Restructuring U.S. Strategic Nuclear Forces. Arms Control Association, Updated October 2007.

[123] Mark Thompson, "Nuclear Triad Warfare," *Time Magazine*, October 18, 2011.

---

what types of bomber weapons, the United States needs to bolster its conventional long-range strike capability. There is little, if any, discussion about the role that bombers may play in either nuclear deterrence, or, if deterrence fails, in the launch of U.S. nuclear weapons. It is not surprising that some in the Air Force and Pentagon and some outside government have questioned the continuing need for nuclear-capable bombers.[124]

The Obama Administration has indicated that the United States will retain 400 deployed ICBMs under the New START Treaty. Each will be equipped with a single warhead. Analysts have often argued, and the 2010 Nuclear Posture Review affirmed, that single-warhead ICBMs bolster crisis stability, and discourage efforts by an adversary to launch a disarming first strike, because the cost of the strike, as measured by the number of attacking warheads, would exceed the benefits, as measured by the number of warheads destroyed. Moreover, these missiles will remain deployed at three ICBM bases.

Some analysts outside government have called for reductions in or even the elimination of the U.S. ICBM force. Some have argued that the Air Force could save up to $360 million per year if it reduced the ICBM force to 300 missiles.[125] Others have noted that, under the current financial pressures, the Air Force may not be able to afford a new ICBM after 2030. Moreover, even if the financial pressures did not exist, some argue the Air Force should eliminate the ICBM force because it no longer serves U.S. national security needs. For example, in a study published in May 2012,[126] the Global Zero Organization argued for the elimination of the ICBM force because it views these missiles as dangerous and destabilizing in the current security environment. It noted that "ICBMs can only support nuclear wartime operations against Russia" and that current-generation ICBMs "fired from the existing bases, on their minimum energy trajectories," have to overfly Russia and China or fly near Russia to reach targets in potentially adversarial countries. It contends that, if U.S. missiles fly over or near Russia on their way to more southerly targets in Iran or Syria, Russia might be confused by ambiguous attack indications and might then launch its own retaliatory attack against the United States. Second, the report asserted that, because ICBMs are based in fixed silos that are vulnerable to destruction in an attack, they must depend heavily upon "launch on warning" to survive and retaliate in some scenarios. As a result, according to the report, ICBMs exacerbate the risk that the United States might launch its weapons on false warning.

Analysts who support the continued deployment of U.S. ICBMs disputed many of the assertions outlined in the Global Zero report. First, they noted that, although each individual ICBM silo may be vulnerable to destruction if targeted by several incoming warheads, an attack that threatened to destroy the entire U.S. ICBM force would have to consist of hundreds, if not thousands of attacking warheads.[127] This is because the United States maintains nearly 450 ICBM silos

---

[124] See, for example, Dr. Dana J. Johnson, Dr. Christopher J. Bowie, and Dr. Robert P. Haffa, *Triad, Dyad, Monad? Shaping the U.S. Nuclear Force for the Future*, Mitchell Institute for Airpower Studies, Washington, DC, November 2009.

[125] Daryl G. Kimball, "Defuse the Exploding Costs of Nuclear Weapons," *Arms Control Today*, December 2012, p. 4.

[126] Global Zero U.S. Nuclear Policy Commission, *Modernizing U.S. Nuclear Strategy, Force Structure, and Posture*, Global Zero, Washington, DC, May 2012, herein after referred to as the Global Zero Report. http://dl.dropbox.com/u/6395109/GZ%20US%20Nuclear%20Policy%20Commission%20Report.pdf.

[127] See, for example, Senate ICBM Coalition, *The Long Pole of the Nuclear Umbrella*, A White Paper on the Criticality of the Intercontinental Ballistic Missile to the United States Security, Washington, DC, November 2009. See also, Peter Huessy, "In Defense of the Nuclear Triad." Defense One, October 18, 2013, http://www.defenseone.com/ideas/2013/10/defense-nuclear-triad/72242/?oref=search_Huessy.

hardened against nuclear blast, and an attacker would have to target two or three warheads against each silo to ensure their destruction. Further, because the United States plans to deploy each Minuteman missile with only a single warhead, the attacker would have to expend two to three times as many warheads as he could hope to destroy. This calculation underpins the conclusion, which is widespread among nuclear policy analysts, that single-warhead ICBMs enhance stability and discourage attack because they are not lucrative targets.[128]

The Obama Administration has also indicated that it plans to retain 14 Trident submarines until it begins retiring the Ohio-class SSBNs in the late 2020s. Moreover, the New START Treaty allows the United States to continue to reduce the warheads on each missile. It also allows the United States to eliminate some of the launch tubes by simply removing the gas generators that assist in the launch of the missiles. As a result, the United States will have a significant amount of flexibility in apportioning warheads among its SSBNs, and will not have to eliminate any submarines to meet the new START limits. Moreover, the Navy does not plan to alter the basic structure of its Trident fleet; it will continue to deploy its submarines at two bases, with a portion of the fleet deployed in the Atlantic Ocean and a portion deployed in the Pacific Ocean. As a result, with its ability to remain invulnerable to detection and attack, and with the increasing accuracy and reliability of its missiles and warheads, the Trident fleet will continue to represent the "backbone" of the U.S. nuclear force.

Some argue that the United States should reduce the size of its SLBM fleet and retain only 8 or 10 submarines. They argue that this reduction now, and the future acquisition of fewer replacement submarines, could save the Navy $6 billion-$7 billion over the next 10 years.[129] They also note that this change need not reduce the number of operational warheads on SLBMs, because the United States would deploy each submarine with 24 missiles, rather than the 20 planned under New START, and could increase the number of warheads on each missile. However, with so few submarines, the United States might have to eliminate one of its submarine bases, leaving it with submarines based only in the Atlantic or only in the Pacific Ocean. Or the United States might have to reduce the number of submarines on station, and, therefore, the number of warheads available to the President promptly, at the start of a conflict. These changes may not be consistent with current submarine operations and employment plans. President Obama and the U.S. military may want to consider the implications of these basing, operational, and policy changes, *before* deciding whether or not to reduce to 1,000 warheads, as opposed to choosing the warhead number first *then* deciding later how to base and operate the remaining nuclear forces.

The Cost of Nuclear Weapons

When the Obama Administration submitted the 1251 report to the Senate during the New START ratification process, it indicated that it expected to spend around $210 billion over the next 10 years (2011-2021) to maintain and modernize the U.S. nuclear arsenal. This total, however, did not include most of the costs of producing and procuring the next generation of submarines, bombers, and missiles, as these activities would occur after the time frame contained in the report. Moreover, it became evident, as Congress reviewed the Administration's plans to modernize the nuclear enterprise, that it was difficult, if not impossible, to determine how much the United

---

[128] See, for example, the comments of General Larry Welch, before the NDIA and ROA Congressional Breakfast Seminar Series, May 25, 2012, http://www.afa.org/hbs/transcripts/5-25-2012%20Gen%20Larry%20Welch%20v2.pdf.

[129] Daryl G. Kimball, "Defuse the Exploding Costs of Nuclear Weapons," *Arms Control Today*, December 2012, p. 4.

States spent each year on nuclear weapons, as the funding was divided between the Department of Defense and the Department of Energy, and, in many cases, was combined with funding for other, non-nuclear activities. In other words, the United States does not maintain a single, unified budget for nuclear weapons and other nuclear activities.

In response to both the growing concerns about the pending costs of nuclear weapons modernization programs and the confusion about how to calculate the annual costs of the nuclear enterprise, Congress directed the Congressional Budget Office (CBO) to estimate the costs of U.S. plans for operating, maintaining and modernizing nuclear weapons, the delivery systems, and the DOE nuclear weapons complex over the next 10 years. CBO issued its report in late 2013.[130] It found that the United States was likely to spend $355 billion over the next 10 years on its nuclear weapons enterprise. This total included $56 million for command, control, communications, and early warning activities and $59 million for additional costs based on historical cost growth of similar programs. Neither of these categories had been included in the Administration's estimate in 2010. When CBO considered the same categories as the Administration, it estimated 10-year spending of $241 million, a number close to the estimate provided by the Administration.

According to CBO, around $89 billion of its $355 billion total over the next 10 years would go to the modernization programs through 2023. As with the Administration's estimate, the CBO estimate did not include procurement costs for most of these programs, as these would occur in the later 2020s and 2030s. The CBO study noted, however, that annual spending on would increase from a total of around $18 billion in FY2014 to an average of $29 billion from 2021 to 2023 and that spending was "likely to continue to grow after 2023 as production begins on replacement systems."[131] This result indicates that the United States could spend at least $30 billion per year on the nuclear weapons enterprise as it completes its modernization programs. This estimate is consistent with others that have been presented by organizations outside government. For example, in January 2014, analysts at the James Martin Center for Nonproliferation Studies estimated that the United States might spend 1 trillion dollars, or an average of just over $30 billion per year, over the next 30 years, to modernize its nuclear enterprise.[132] In addition, in a briefing prepared in May 2013, the Air Force estimated that the investments in nuclear modernization programs would peak in between 2025 and 2035, at approximately $30 billion per year.[133]

Safety, Security, and Management Issues

In late August 2007, a B-52 bomber based in Minot, ND, took off on flight to Barksdale Air Force Base in Louisiana. The bomber carried 12 air-launched cruise missiles that were slated for retirement at Barksdale. As a result of a series of errors and missteps in the process of removing the missiles from storage and loading them on the bombers, six of the missiles carried live

---

[130] Congressional Budget Office, *Projected Costs of U.S. Nuclear Forces, 2014-2023*, Washington, DC, December 2013, http://www.cbo.gov/sites/default/files/cbofiles/attachments/12-19-2013-NuclearForces.pdf.

[131] Ibid., p. 2.

[132] Jon B. Wolfsthal, Jeffrey Lewis, and Marc Quint, *The Trillion Dollar Nuclear Triad*, James Martin Center for Nonproliferation Studies, Monterey, CA, January 2014, http://cns.miis.edu/opapers/pdfs/140107_trillion_dollar_nuclear_triad.pdf.

[133] For a copy of General Kowalski's briefing slides, see http://www.fas.org/programs/ssp/nukes/nuclearweapons/AFGSC-CommandBrief-May2013.pdf.

nuclear warheads, instead of the dummy warheads that were installed on missiles heading for retirement. This episode led to a series of studies and reviews by the Air Force that identified the source of the episode and identified a number of steps the Air Force should take to improve its handling of nuclear weapons.[134]

In early June 2008, Secretary of Defense Robert Gates requested the resignations of the Secretary of the Air Force, Michael Wynne, and the Chief of Staff of the Air Force, General Michael Mosely, from their positions, at least in part, due to concerns about that shortcomings in the Air Force's handling of nuclear weapons "resulted from an erosion of performance standards within the involved commands and a lack of effective Air Force leadership oversight."[135] Secretary Gates appointed a task force, led by former Secretary of Defense and Energy James Schlesinger, to provide "independent advice on the organizational, procedural and policy improvements necessary to ensure that the highest levels of accountability and control are maintained in the department's stewardship of nuclear weapons, delivery vehicles, sensitive components and basing procedures."[136]

Several of the studies that reviewed this event concluded that the Air Force leadership had lost its focus on the nuclear mission as it diverted resources to more pressing missions related to the ongoing conflicts in Iraq and Afghanistan. As a result the "nuclear enterprise" had been allowed to atrophy, with evident declines in morale, cohesion, and capability.[137] These reports suggested that the United States restore its focus on the nuclear mission and repair long-standing and often-identified deficiencies in manpower and training programs for crews that maintain and service nuclear weapons and operate nuclear-capable bombers. The studies identified a number of organizational changes to achieve these goals. For example, the Air Force has created a new Global Strike Command, based at Barksdale Air Force Base, that is responsible for both the ICBM force and the nuclear-capable bombers. This organization began its operations in early 2009. The Air Force has also established a new headquarters office in the Pentagon that will monitor and manage the resources and policies dedicated to the nuclear mission. The Air Force also altered its inspection program and its expectations for achievement during these inspections.

In a study published in April 2011, the Defense Science Board reviewed and evaluated the changes Air Force had made in its nuclear weapons enterprise.[138] The report noted that Air Force leadership "has taken decisive action to correct deficiencies, reinvigorate, and further strengthen the Air Force Nuclear Enterprise."[139] At the same time, though, the study noted that some of the "extraordinary measures" taken in response to the earlier lapses could have negative impacts if they are extended beyond the "period of urgent need." This problem was particularly evident in

---

[134] See, for example, The Defense Science Board Permanent Task Force on Nuclear Weapons Surety. Report on the Unauthorized Movement of Nuclear Weapons. February 2008.

[135] Nuclear Lapses Trigger Ouster of Top U.S. Air Force Officials. Global Security Newswire. June 6, 2008.

[136] U.S. Department of Defense. Office of the Assistant Secretary of Defense (Public Affairs). Department of Defense Announces Task Force on Nuclear Weapons Management. June 12, 2008.

[137] See, for example, United States Air Force, *Reinvigorating the Air Force Nuclear Enterprise*, Prepared by the Air Force Nuclear Task Force, Washington, DC, October 24, 2008, http://www.af mil/shared/media/document/AFD-081024-073.pdf. See also, Report of the Secretary of Defense Task Force on DOD Nuclear Weapons Management (the Schlesinger Commission), *Phase I: The Air Force's Nuclear Mission,* Washington, DC September 2008. http://www.defenselink mil/pubs/Phase_I_Report_Sept_10.pdf.

[138] Defense Science Board Permanent Task Force on Nuclear Weapons Surety, *Independent Assessment of The Air force Nuclear Enterprise*, Washington, DC, April 2011. http://www.acq.osd mil/dsb/reports/NWS_2010.pdf.

[139] Ibid., p. 16.

the areas of oversight and inspection. The study reported that there has been "intense attention to the issue of accountability and control of nuclear weapons-related materials." But the numerous and overlapping inspections have become so frequent and invasive that the units may not have the time or resources to correct deficiencies found during the many inspections. As a result, the task force concluded that the intense level of inspections and exercises had become counterproductive by interfering with the normal rhythm of operations at the wings.[140]

Several incidents that have occurred in 2013 and early 2014 have raised new concerns about the capabilities and morale of ICBM launch officers. For example, press reports from May 2013 noted that the Air Force had removed 17 launch officers from duty at Minot Air Force Base and had sent them for additional training after they earned low scores on an inspection in March.[141] In August, a missile unit at Malmstrom Air Force Base also received a failing grade on an inspection. Air Force officials expressed concern about these results, but noted that they remained confident in the capabilities of Air Force nuclear officers. After the incident in Minot, some saw the commander's response, and the remedial action, as a sign of progress in the force, because problems were identified and corrected on site. Others have noted that unsatisfactory results in inspections may be the result of higher expectations, and do not necessarily indicate deeper problems. Others, however, view the low scores on inspections as a symptom of continuing problems in the force.

Two other incidents in September and October 2013 also raised concerns about the U.S. nuclear enterprise, even though they did not affect the safety or security of the nuclear force. In September, Vice Admiral Timothy Giardina, the second-in-command at STRATCOM, was suspended after an investigation into the use of counterfeit gambling chips. In October, Major General Michael Carey, the Commander of 20th Air Force, which is responsible for the entire ICBM fleet, was reassigned following an investigation into "personal misbehavior."[142]

In January 2014, press reports indicated that nuclear launch officers at Malmstrom Air Force Base had been implicated in a drug investigation. While investigating this charge, the Air Force discovered that 34 of launch officers may have been cheating on their monthly proficiency exams. In response to this event, Secretary of Defense Hagel ordered an internal review of nuclear weapons personnel issues and commissioned another outside study of morale and effectiveness in the nuclear enterprise. As this review has proceeded, the Air Force has questioned whether some officers in the nuclear force may be experiencing "burnout" and boredom in a mission that seems connected to an earlier time and whether the tense atmosphere created by the frequent testing and inspection regimes has created incentives to cheat to produce perfect scores.[143]

The Air Force has responded to these problems with plans to increase funding, raise pay levels, introduce new management positions, modify the testing process, and raise morale among Air Force ICBM officers. Many of these plans are designed to highlight the high value that Air Force places on the ICBM mission and to convince airmen that their leaders value their effort and

---

[140] Ibid., pp. 22-23.

[141] Robert Burns, "Air Force Sidelines 17 ICBM launch officers: commander cites 'rot' within system," *Associated Press*, May 8, 2013.

[142] "Air Force Fires General In Charge Of Nuclear Missiles," *Los Angeles Times*, October 11, 2013.

[143] R. Jeffrey Smith, "Aiming High: Boredom, Drugs, Low Morale. The millennials of the U.S. nuclear missile corps are struggling to stay on high alert for a nuclear Armageddon," *Slate*, April 2014.

accomplishment. At the same time, though, the changes will require additional funding, and the Air Force will need to request increases in its budget in an era of fiscal restraint to follow through on these initiatives.

While the Air Force has worked to increase the level of attention and accountability for its nuclear weapons after these incidents, others analysts found different lessons in the lapses. Some saw the decline of the Air Force nuclear enterprise as an inevitable part of the declining role of nuclear weapons in U.S. national security strategy and argued that the United States should extend the process by further reducing its nuclear arsenal and removing greater numbers of weapons from the operational force. For example, some suggested that the evident weaknesses in the Air Force's procedures argued for removing nuclear weapons from the whole of the bomber fleet.[144] Congress may address concerns about these issues, and review possible changes in command structures and security procedures, as it reviews nuclear weapons policies and programs during its next session.

Author Contact Information

Amy F. Woolf
Specialist in Nuclear Weapons Policy
awoolf@crs.loc.gov, 7-2379

---

[144] Kristensen, Hans. Nuclear Safety and the Saga of the Missing Bent Spear. Federation of the American Scientists. February 22, 2008. http://www.fas.org/blog/ssp/2008/02/nuclear_safety_and_the_saga_ab.php.

www.ingramcontent.com/pod-product-compliance
Lightning Source LLC
Chambersburg PA
CBHW080628290526
45790CB00007B/2966